Ethics and Responsibility in Finance

From the mid-1970s until the crisis in 2007, the world of finance enjoyed thirty euphoric years as the general public, businesses and governments put their blind trust in financial techniques, professions and institutions. Shaken up by a structural crisis and a crisis of legitimacy, today's financial sector can no longer afford to avoid the issues summed up by the key question: what is next for the role of ethics and responsibility in finance? Many see an unbridgeable gap between ethics and responsibility and financial practice. *Ethics and Responsibility in Finance* paves the way for the dialogue that is needed in order to solve the current problems and allow the return of a refined ethical thinking in the financial sector.

This book opens with an in-depth analysis of the operational implications of two key notions: ethics and responsibility. It then addresses ethical dilemmas that are characteristic to each of the three actors involved in any financial transaction. This begins with the discussion of the dilemmas of the ultimate owner of funds: the individual or collective saver, as in the case of pension funds. The analysis then turns to financial intermediaries such as banks, insurance companies, asset managers and consultants, who work in a web of different loyalties. Finally, the dilemmas of the user of funds are addressed – the household taking a mortgage, an enterprise or a public authority which borrows – all of which have to be clear on the reasons and values driving their decisions.

This volume is of great interest to those who study banking, corporate finance and ethics philosophy.

Paul H. Dembinski holds the Chair of International Strategy and Competition at Switzerland's University of Fribourg. He has a doctorate in political economy (1982) from the University of Geneva, where he began his teaching career, later (1991) becoming a tenured associate professor at the University of Fribourg. In 1996 he launched the Observatoire de la Finance Foundation in Geneva (www.obsfin.ch) with the aim of encouraging the financial sector to take more account of the common good. He is still its director, and is chair of the international Ethics & Trust in Finance Prize, which will be awarded for the sixth time in 2017. He also edits the bilingual journal *Finance & the Common Good/Finance & Bien Commun*. Paul H. Dembinski is on the board of directors of Rentes Genevoises (public annuity company), which he has chaired since 2012.

Routledge Focus on Economics and Finance

The fields of economics are constantly expanding and evolving. This growth presents challenges for readers trying to keep up with the latest important insights. Routledge Focus on Economics and Finance presents short books on the latest big topics, linking in with the most cutting edge economics research.

Individually, each title in the series provides coverage of a key academic topic, whilst collectively the series forms a comprehensive collection across the whole spectrum of economics.

1   **International Macroeconomics for Business and Political Leaders**
    John E. Marthinsen

2   **Ethics and Responsibility in Finance**
    Paul H. Dembinski

Ethics and Responsibility in Finance

Paul H. Dembinski
Translated by Kevin Cook

LONDON AND NEW YORK

First published 2017 by Routledge

2 Park Square, Milton Park, Abingdon, Oxfordshire OX14 4RN

52 Vanderbilt Avenue, New York, NY 10017

Routledge is an imprint of the Taylor & Francis Group, an informa business

First issued in paperback 2020

British Library Cataloguing in Publication Data
A catalogue record for this book is available from the British Library

Library of Congress Cataloging in Publication Data
A catalog record for this book has been requested

ISBN: 978-1-138-63790-0 (hbk)
ISBN: 978-0-367-60743-2 (pbk)

Typeset in Times New Roman
by Swales & Willis Ltd, Exeter, Devon, UK

Contents

1   Introduction: why does finance need ethics?   1
    1.1   *Permanent (or structural) reasons 3*
    1.2   *Accidental (or cyclical) reasons 4*

2   Finance and ethics: a twofold update   8
    2.1   *Can finance be defined? 8*
    2.2   *Finance and money: the strength of promises 10*
    2.3   *The multimodal causality toolbox 11*
    2.4   *The causes of financialisation 11*
    2.5   *How to define ethics? 17*
    2.6   *Responsibility 19*
    2.7   *The dilemma: the locus of ethics 21*
    2.8   *The four dimensions of an ethical assessment 23*

3   The fund holder's ethical dilemmas: savers and *rentiers*   27
    3.1   *From non-consumption to savings 27*
    3.2   *Intergenerational assets 29*
    3.3   *Implementing the societal responsibility of the*
          saver: 'sustainable finance' 31
    3.4   *Forced savings: life insurance and pension funds 33*
    3.5   *Interest: the (forbidden) fruit of savings 34*
    3.6   *Gambling or financing? 35*
    3.7   *Asset and risk management institutions 37*
    3.8   *The role of savings at macroeconomic level 38*

4   The ethical dilemmas facing fund users: public or
    private debtors and investors   40
    4.1   *The roots of promises and households' commitments 40*
    4.2   *Risk and business financing 42*

vi   *Contents*

4.3   Business financing: the leverage dilemma 43
4.4   The discount rate dilemma 44
4.5   Public fund users 45
4.6   The ethical aspects of information asymmetry 46
4.7   Accounting conventions and the importance
      of judgement 47
4.8   The usury rate 49
4.9   Ways out when things go wrong: the macro level 50
4.10 The Jubilee project: keeping financial due dates
      under control 51

5   **Ethical dilemmas in financial intermediation**   53
5.1   Banks or markets: an alternative made
      irrelevant by globalisation 53
5.2   Advise, prescribe or sell? 56
5.3   Financial innovation: cui bono? 59
5.4   The quality of prices: insider trading,
      market rigging and dark pools 60
5.5   Volatility and risk transfer 63

6   **New avenues for action**   65
6.1   Curbing expectations and aspirations in finance 66
6.2   Enhancing the importance of personal relationships 68
6.3   Simplifying the way finance works 69
6.4   Teaching finance differently 71
6.5   Ethics as a goal 72

Bibliography   74
Index   77

1 Introduction

Why does finance need ethics?

In autumn 1998, under pressure from the American authorities, the world's leading financial players rescued a failing hedge fund called Long-Term Capital Management, which had become systemically important and was run by financial geniuses including two Nobel prizewinners. Ten years before the start of the crisis in 2007, this was the moment when world finance entered a period of upheaval that would shake it to its foundations. Individual events such as the collapse of Enron in 2001 or the 2003 Parmalat scandal, thought at the time to be mere incidents, were followed by shocks that reached the very heart of the financial world. Since then, systemically important events have continued to threaten global finance – and the whole of the world economy.

Although the timeline of 'the crisis' may be tedious to recall, it has certainly not been forgotten: the subprime mortgage crisis, the bankruptcy and bailout of various key players, the sovereign-debt crisis, the repeated crises in the eurozone, the unconventional policies pursued by the central banks and more recently, the historically and persistently low interest rates which may prove to be a time bomb in financial operators' balance sheets.

In 2017, a return to the pre-2007 status quo seems less and less likely or feasible; but it is still far from clear how things will eventually turn out. Nonetheless, it is obvious to some observers – although not everyone would agree – that a systemic transformation process is taking place, especially as regards the role, position and societal legitimacy of finance. There are many mutually reinforcing pressures on the financial sector: economic (structural and cyclical), regulatory, political and media-driven. These pressures reflect a now widespread feeling in society that for decades – with the world turning a blind eye – the financial sector has cheerfully flouted the moral and ethical norms that were supposed to keep it under control.

The long list of penalties and lawsuits since 2007 has cast an often harsh public light on the behaviour and actions of financial players who yesterday were still seen as role models; and public outrage – which according to the

Petit Robert French dictionary is the main ingredient of any scandal – now condemns the financial sector and expresses the general feeling of having been taken for a ride. A bitter sense of betrayed trust between finance, the economy and society has spread throughout the world, forcing the sector to reconsider its economic and societal status, as well as its business models.

Such a highly charged atmosphere lends itself to often glib ethical or moral judgements. More fundamentally, however, long-ignored ethical questions about finance are once again meaningful and legitimate. These questions are now being raised by the sector itself, by the media and by intellectuals, by academic and professional training centres, by political and regulatory bodies and by civil society. They concern both the profound meaning of finance and the ways in which it is operates. Quite clearly, the various aspects of ethics are the focus of the many pressures now facing the financial sector.[1]

Since the end of the 'Thirty Glorious Years', which were brought to an abrupt halt by the crises of the 1970s, finance has grown increasingly important in the global economy, spurred on by euphoric promises of new growth horizons opened up by financial techniques and models. That is why the three decades from the mid-1970s to 2007 can now be dubbed the 'Thirty Euphoric Years'. During this period the general public, businesses and governments (regardless of political colour) put their blind trust in financial techniques, professions and institutions. The present crisis has put an end to these three decades of collective blindness. A shocked world has realised not just how disproportionate the previous developments were, but above all that they took place in a vacuum, beyond outside control, whether political or ethical. During the Thirty Euphoric Years, people's sense of prudent and meaningful endeavour was dulled, and ethical questions were pushed into the background. When the bubble burst in 2007 amid market failures and repeated scandals, it was a rude awakening that created a still unallayed sense of betrayal.

The purpose of this book is not to rediagnose the financial crisis[2] – which has been discussed in great detail elsewhere – but to encourage a return to ethical thinking in keeping with post-2007 finance. Shaken up by a structural crisis and a crisis of legitimacy, today's financial sector can no longer afford to avoid the issues summed up by the key question 'Ethics and responsibility in finance: what next?'

Although ethical questioning pertains of course to all human activity, it must be adapted to the conditions in which each of these activities takes place; and finance is no exception. Account must therefore be taken of recent developments and the associated specific issues. In short, there are two kinds of reasons why the ethical questioning relating to finance needs to be up dated (1) *permanent (or structural)* reasons relating to the timeless nature of finance and the ethical questions that it has always raised – but that were forgotten in recent decades; and (2) *accidental* (or *cyclical)* reasons, which depend on the specific conditions of modern finance, as revealed by the crisis.

1.1 Permanent (or structural) reasons

Over the centuries, moralists have focused on finance, presenting at least five good reasons for which, as in all human activities, finance is subject to moral law:

- The *first* is that finance uses money as one of its main resources; and money is a social institution that is loaded with meaning and arouses particularly strong emotions sometimes verging on religious worship. Especially now that the power and seductiveness of money are at their height, activities involving such a sensitive object cannot ignore ethical considerations for long.
- The *second* is that another of the resources used by finance is time – or rather the future, and specifically other people's futures. All financial assets are geared to future events, and all modern financial transactions depend on a monetary assessment of the future – a future full of uncertainties and risks, for which finance offers commitments and guarantees. The problems of evaluating the unknown, the acceptable level of guarantee and of remuneration and/or distribution of risks are essentially ethical ones, which have been discussed by the main religious and cultural traditions over the centuries.[3]
- The *third* concerns finance's third resource: trust. The money used by finance is largely in the form of savings, that is, reserves built up to meet future needs. Such reserves cannot be brought (or brought back) into circulation without a minimum of trust and loyalty between the parties; and, sometimes implicitly, both trust and loyalty involve ethics.
- The *fourth* is that finance is an intermediary activity. Those who work in the financial sector earning their living by handling other people's futures, trust and money, performing transactions between their clients' often conflicting interests. In doing so, they always have an eye to their own remuneration and interests. This raises the eminently ethical question of how, and at what level, they should be remunerated.
- The *fifth* concerns the purely quantitative language that is typically used by the financial sector. The predominance of numbers, now made virtual by information technology, tends to conceal their real – social and economic – meanings and implications. There is therefore a danger that financial calculations may erase reality in favour of figures that

are solely generated by arithmetical manipulation. Numbers disguise the rough edges and gaps in reality by postulating an ideal world in which all things are perfectly divisible and perfectly interchangeable. Ethics forces us to look beyond this virtual screen and get back to reality, ensuring that reality can never be entirely replaced by numbers, however useful and convenient they may seem.

1.2 Accidental (or cyclical) reasons

If, as we have just seen, finance always needs an ethical framework, why is this nowadays so manifestly lacking? There is no shortage of technical literature on the reasons for the financial crisis; but none of it explains *why* ethics has come to be lacking. Five more accidental reasons, related to the present situation, spring to mind, in addition to the structural ones mentioned above:

- The *first* is the claim of modern theory of finance's to be based on scientific – and hence objective – foundations, and thus to be purely technical as opposed to philosophical. Given this claim of the theory to be scientific, contemporary finance grew on purely positivistic grounds in symbiosis with practice and almost without reference to epistemology or ethics. It was in the 1970s that modern theory of finance ('market finance') began to take control of reality, redesigning the organisation of public and private institutions and professional practices. These changes reflected intellectual breakthroughs that occurred in American universities labs and think tanks twenty years earlier. They would be amply rewarded with Nobel prizes decades later – that is well after the modern financial *Weltanschauung*[4] had become firmly established as a universal frame of reference. The founding fathers of this new science, such as Harry Markowitz, Merton Miller, Franco Modigliani, Eugene Fama and William Sharpe, gave finance a new rationality based on the risk/reward paradigm, and a suitable toolbox.

  In the light of economic success and purely technical performance, the ethical questions that in one way or another had always been present in traditional finance were now systematically ignored. The unparalleled performances that validated the paradigm left less and less reason for such questions to be asked. In a context of prosperity, neither specialised institutions nor individual operators felt inclined to look at potentially troublesome issues. The blind enthusiasm fed by performance overcame prudence, and hence ethics; and so this enthusiasm gradually turned into euphoria. The recent developments in financial theory and practice thus largely occurred in the absence of ethical thinking.

- The *second reason* for the lack of ethics concerns the digital technology that both allowed and accompanied the development of finance. Breakthroughs in this area further exacerbated the natural propensity of finance to focus on the digital and the virtual, and now on a global scale. Whole generations of financial operators thus became, in Robert Reich's phrase, perfect 'symbol manipulators',[5] without caring about the foundations and the spatial or social consequences of the processes involved. The technology they used literally cut them off from the realities behind the digital bytes on their screens. Comfortably seated at their displays, the symbol manipulators were not encouraged by such an environment to ask themselves ethical questions; and they eventually lost their instinct to do so. The socioeconomic realities that finance ultimately refers to thus became less visible and more remote, to be replaced by the dynamics of symbols in the virtual space of technology and intellectual sophistication. A working environment that is cut off from reality may lead to a kind of ethical autism. To the extent that they survived at all, ethical considerations also became more abstract.

- The *third reason* that contributed to the progressive silencing of ethical reflexes was the size and complexity of the institutions involved. Size and complexity increased the aforementioned virtualising impact of the new technologies. During the Thirty Euphoric Years, world finance became increasingly concentrated in the hands of a few dozen global operators, for whom specialisation and internal fragmentation of tasks were standard practice.[6] As a result, many employees no longer had an overall view of financial products and services, or their value to clients. In the absence of contact with clients and an overall view of the services provided, many employees fell victim to an 'ethical alienation' syndrome that culminated in disengagement.[7] This was enhanced by constant references to 'market forces' whose power supposedly relegated individuals to a marginal state of helplessness, and ultimately relieved them of all responsibility. It is hardly surprising that many operators ended up losing their sense of responsibility in the face of events which, by theory-driven definition, were beyond their control, but to which their behaviour and decisions contributed at the margin.

- The *fourth reason* for the present collapse of ethics is the globalisation of institutions and activities. Finance – especially in its more sophisticated aspects – rapidly became a cosmopolitan space in which cultural and moral frameworks were replaced by patterns of behaviour that supposedly ensured a minimum of mutual understanding. Attempts to develop 'corporate cultures' scarcely made up for the disappearance of the cultural and religious frames of reference shared by teams working within institutions. However, as the crisis made only too clear, ethics was always the 'poor relation' in such efforts, and has continued to be overlooked by corporate cultures. Since 2012, public regulators have taken an increasing interest in the corporate cultures of major private operators, which they see as a serious risk to the financial system.[8]

- The *fifth reason* is the macrosocietal impact of contemporary finance which, owing to its omnipresence, has acquired systemic importance. As an economic sector, finance is today a source not only of opportunities and promises of efficiency and performance, but also of systemic risk. This new factor is associated with moral hazard, and so must be analysed in terms of ethics.

In short, ethics and prudence were sorely lacking during the Thirty Euphoric Years, because the conditions surrounding the birth of modern finance dulled private, public and academic players' traditional sense of ethics. What we now therefore need is a two-way update.

- In finance – in the broadest sense – we need an overall ethical update before it is too late.
- In ethics, we need to step up existing efforts and take account of the context of modern finance so as to discover, or rediscover, the contemporary relevance of traditional questions, so as to identify the new questions that are specific to the present day.[9]

This book sets out to smooth the way for the two-way update that is needed in order to solve the current problems and allow a return of a refined ethical thinking in the financial sector. Many actors and observers see an unbridgeable gap between ethics and responsibility and financial practice – even a contradiction in terms, or 'oxymoron', between ethics and finance.

The book comprises five chapters besides the introduction. The first chapter reviews the basic notions of 'finance', 'ethics' and 'responsibility' and identifies the interfaces between them. It outlines the main features of finance during the Thirty Euphoric Years, and recalls the historical dimension of the major ethical debates on the subject.

The next three chapters look in succession at the ethical dilemmas encountered by the main groups of actors in the financial sector:

- ultimate fund holders: individual or group savers;
- ultimate fund users: investing entrepreneurs, consumers or property owners, and public bodies;
- providers of financial services in the broad sense: intermediaries responsible for informing, advising or taking the place of ultimate fund users or holders.

Each of the chapters on dilemmas will ask ethical questions on three levels:

a   *the macro level*, at which the legislative framework is created. Here the questions concern social ethics, the tasks and functions of money and finance, and what is or is not permissible in the financial sector;
b   *the meso level*, the level of institutions, markets, products and professions. Here we will see ethical questions relating to how finance and the financial professions are conducted, as well as relationships with users. They concern professions (codes of ethics) and public or private financial institutions. These are expressed through the institutions' cultures, organisation and internal regulations;
c   *the micro level*, the level of individual actors, savers, managers, professionals and those in charge of large and small organisations. All these individuals, in their various roles, face ethical questions and dilemmas.

The final chapter suggests a number of avenues for future action that will enable finance to regain its social legitimacy – but these will involve adaptations, some of them fundamental.

Notes

1 See Group of 30, *Banking Conduct and Culture, A Call for Sustained and Comprehensive Reform*, Washington, July 2015, http://group30.org/images/uploads/publications/G30_BankingConductandCulture.pdf.
2 See Paul H. Dembinski, *Finance: Servant or Deceiver? Financialisation at Crossroads*, Palgrave Macmillan, London, 2008 (the original French version can be downloaded free of charge from www.obsfin.ch).
3 The scholastics believed that loans should be free from such 'speculation' on the future, for they are not supposed to bear interest. Similarly, both Islam and Judaism prohibit lending with interest, but not loans. This raises the question of whether an interest-free loan can be considered part of finance in the modern sense.
4 World view.
5 Robert Reich, *The Work of Nations*, Vintage Press, New York, 1992.
6 In 2011 the Financial Stability Board began publishing an annual list of systemically important financial institutions. Last updated in November 2014, the list now includes 30 global systemically important banks (G-SIBs). The methodology behind the list combines indicators of the institutions' size, connections and complexity, as well as the relative uniqueness of their infrastructures or services. http://www.fsb.org/2016/11/2016-list-of-global-systemically-important-banks-g-sibs/.
7 See Paul H. Dembinski, *op. cit.*
8 Group of 30 (2015), *op. cit.*
9 Paul H. Dembinski, *op. cit.*; Étienne Perrot, *Refus du risque et catastrophes financières*, Salvator, Paris, 2011; Judith Assouly, *Morale ou Finance? La déontologie dans les pratiques financières*, Les presses de Sciences Po, Paris, 2013. See also the issues of the Observatoire de la Finance journal *Finance & the Common Good* from 1998 to 2013.

2 Finance and ethics
A twofold update

2.1 Can finance be defined?

Of the many definitions of finance in literature, the title of Pierre-Noël Giraud's *Trade in Promises: A Small Treatise on Modern Finance*[1] provides an ideal starting point for the subject of this book. This graphic definition reveals the depth, including the ethical depth, of this field of human endeavour.

To avoid oversimplification, the concise, highly evocative definition of finance as 'trade in promises' should be qualified in three ways:

- First, the word 'promises' should be seen not only in its broadest sense, but should include, in addition to promises (which, as the saying goes, only commit those who listen to them), any kind of commitment or stance in relation to the future. They thus also include formal commitments such as contracts, as well as gambles on potential futures based on personal convictions rather than promises by third parties. Nevertheless, they involve also financial commitments.
- Second, promises, gambles and commitments in the financial sector only concern present or future payments.
- Third, to be complete, the definition of finance should be extended beyond mere trade in promises to include their production and management.

This means that finance should be defined as production and management of, and trade in, promises, commitments and gambles relating to present and future payments.

Each of the terms in the concise definition provided here points to a particular aspect of finance: 'production, management and trade' concern the technical, organisational side; 'promises' refers to the psychological, emotional aspect, as well as the legal, formal dimension associated with the notion of commitment between two parties. The term 'gambles', in the sense of betting on possible futures without being able to influence them, shows that speculation is an integral part of finance. Finally, this definition also includes the monetary dimension, and thus shows how close money and finance are to each other. The use and management of idle cash balances are the necessary, inseparable counterpart of finance.

The basic unit of finance is thus the transaction or the contract relating – in the vast majority of cases – to (a) immediate payment and (b) a commitment to, or a promise or an expectation of (as in the case of a gamble), future payment. Such an implicit or explicit contract creates interdependence between the two parties, who will remain linked until the contract ends. Between the moment when the first payments are effected and the moment when the contracts end, the documents certifying the promises, gambles and commitments become financial assets. Some of these assets are likely to live their own life beyond the direct control of the initial parties and thus can possibly be used as a basis for creating other types of assets, such as derivatives or 'structured' or 'synthetic' products.

The definition of finance used here allows us to identify four segments in contemporary finance, each subject to its own logic of action:

a   production of promises: the set of decisions whereby each individual actor decides how to balance the state of his short-term need for monetary resources and his own propensity to take on and formalise more long-term commitments. In technical terms, such activities involve managing the liability side of non-financial actors' balance sheets;

b   purchase, holding and selling of promises, commitments and gambles made by others. Holders of other people's promises seek to adjust their positions to available opportunities in order to control both risk/reward and due dates. Such activities involve managing the financial part of the asset side of non-financial actors' balance sheets;

c   the set of financial institutions and their interactions that ensure intermediation between the producers and the ultimate beneficiaries of promises, gambles and commitments. This segment includes products, institutions and markets, as well as less classic intermediaries ('shadow banking'), such as investment funds, and suppliers of derivatives and structured products.

d   supervision and regulation whereby the community, embodied by the government, imposes a legislative and regulatory framework on each of the aforementioned activities or institutions. A growing share of national regulatory activities is inspired by, or directly derived from, decisions reached by the European Union or at global level, for instance by the Financial Stability Board.

The first two segments, producing and holding promises and gambles, are governed by the logic of use of financial services, in which financial assets are merely instruments for achieving non-financial goals. The same applies to development of the family, protection of retirement income, growth of businesses or improvement in the supply of infrastructure by public authorities.

In contrast, in the intermediation segment finance is a goal in itself. The logic of selling services prevails there and generates income for the professionals of intermediation. As for regulatory logic – the fourth segment – its task is to ensure that finance contributes to the prosperity and harmony of the community, and that it develops without undermining public trust. Today this task mainly focuses on achieving a fair distribution of risks and rewards between financial actors and maintaining financial stability at the macro level.

2.2 Finance and money: the strength of promises

Finance – trade in promises – is not separate from money, for financial promises imply payment. In modern societies the management of money is based on public logic, in which the monetary function is performed by the central bank. Society thus makes promises about its own survival. Fiduciary money is the – less and less – tangible expression of these promises which together reflect money users' shared faith in their future as a payment community. Money is therefore a promise about a society's future economic activity rather than a commitment to the assets of its central bank (as it was in the days of the dollar standard and its variants). Beyond this promise, fiduciary money has no intrinsic value. Things were different in the days of gold-backed money, for gold has a value in itself that is also acknowledged outside the payment community.[2]

In the light of this definition, finance is the place where a private promise or a commitment is traded for money, that is, a public promise. Apart from the exchange-rate constraint, the difference between modern fiduciary money and financial assets is based on the perceived soundness of the underlying promises: a community's institutional promise that it will survive, and an individual's or a business's private promise to others on the basis of his/its assets or prospects.

As once suggested by Friedrich Hayek,[3] in a world without public money private commitments would have to perform monetary functions. They would do so by submitting, through competition, to the verdict of the market, which would thus determine the value of the various 'signatures' and hence their relative acceptability as means of payment. In this hypothesis, any payment would in fact be a financial transaction, for the goods would be traded for a private commitment.[4]

2.3 The multimodal causality toolbox

'Multimodal causality' refers to an analytical approach that goes back to Aristotle. Whereas modern methodologies give the term 'causality' a very precise meaning based on a direct, mechanical cause-and-effect relationship, the ancient sages included a far broader spectrum of considerations within this term. Aristotle thus focused on the coexistence of a plurality of causes, each operating within its own particular order. The 'multimodal causality' approach enables us to identify every one of the causes – each within its own order – at work in phenomena such as finance and financialisation.

Before applying the approach to financial issues, a classical example will illustrate its power: the creation of statues. Aristotle's views were later adopted and pursued in further depth, particularly by the Thomist tradition.[5]

Why does a statue come into being? Its *material cause* is the pre-existing shapeless block of marble. It is the sculptor's work that turns the marble – the raw material – into a statue. Accordingly, the *formal cause* of the statue is its form as a statue, which henceforth distinguishes it from other blocks of marble. As for the sculptor, he is the *efficient cause* of the statue. It is through his action that the statue, extracted from the block of crude marble, takes shape. In his work the sculptor uses chisels and hammers: these are the *instrumental causes* of the sculpture.

As he works on his block of marble, the artist has in mind a project, an idea, that he seeks to materialise in his sculpture. This idea is the *exemplary cause*, which guides and channels his efforts to achieve an anticipated object. Beyond the projected statue he has in mind, the sculptor is pursuing a higher goal through his work – the *final cause*, which captures the reasons that induce the sculptor to create and work. Several goals may thus coexist: the pursuit of beauty, recognition or money, and so on. All these go beyond, and transcend, the actual sculpture.

As this example shows, multimodal causality is an essentially transdisciplinary approach. It enables things to be combined that current science tends to study in isolation. In the light of the converging beam of causes, we obtain, if not an explanation referring to general laws of physics, at least an overall view of the various facets of a unique phenomenon.

By applying the multimodal causality analysis to finance we can thus distinguish, and at the same time combine, its various dimensions: social, legal and economic, technical, intellectual and ethical.

2.4 The causes of financialisation

In the second half of the twentieth century, finance experienced a meteoric expansion unprecedented in recent history. In the three decades up to 2007, the financial intermediation sector's share of GNP in the leading industrialised countries more than doubled to around 5 to 7 per cent, and over 10 per cent in financial centres such as Luxembourg and Switzerland. During the Thirty Euphoric Years, financial intermediation services thus had to meet growing demand compared with other sectors of the economy. This enthusiasm for finance, its techniques and its products was due to a complex interplay of factors that multimodal causality helps us to understand.

The material cause: the socioeconomic fabric

What is the raw material of finance? In the introduction, three basic ingredients were mentioned: actors' wish to build up their futures by means of promises and commitments; the existence of idle cash balances; and a minimum of trust.

The demutualisation of traditional communities is one of the main recent developments in Western countries. Thus the progressive abandonment of fixed exchange rates in the early 1970s was part of the same phenomenon as the sexual revolution, and was enhanced by consumer society. In the case of exchange rates, or family structure, demutualisation (of villages and neighbourhoods, countries, families or businesses) marked the beginning of an everyone-for-himself era, particularly when it came to the pursuit of future stability and security. Apparent gains in freedom and autonomy were compensated for by – less visible – growth in intertemporal commitments. Although the interplay of credit and savings enabled everyday constraints and interpersonal links to be relaxed, it was set off by stricter demands on intertemporal financial discipline. As a result, both individuals and public bodies exchanged promises and financial commitments regarding their own futures – which, in the process, became subject to increasing constraints or risks.

In premodern communities (clans, villages, families, etc.), future security and management of the associated risks were largely mutualised. The community ensured the survival of each of its members by a blend of cooperation, reciprocity and solidarity as long as the member remained within it.

The increased freedom provided by the liberal project encouraged the individualisation of people's lives, and made financial techniques a toolbox for preparing future security in an everyone-for-himself world. At the macrosocial level, this encouraged the development of finance, which was supposed to maintain, at societal level, a balance between availabilities, commitments and individual promises.

This shift towards the individualisation of commitments was made possible by the growing prosperity of Western society, whose level of accumulated savings continued to rise. Free resources that could be allocated to 'trade in promises' thus became increasingly available starting from 1960s.

During the same period, as interpersonal links weakened and people's futures were demutualised, an almost blind trust in institutional stability was taking root in the Western world – especially after the fall of the Berlin Wall. Against this background, 'trade in promises' was able to flourish unchecked. The now iconic titles of two books symbolise this absolute trust in the irreversibility of globalisation and the stability of institutions: Francis Fukuyama's *The End of History* (1992) and Thomas Friedman's *The World Is Flat* (2005).

The formal cause: from relationships to transactions

The recent changes in society – the raw material of finance – highlight an important paradox that has yet to be analysed in depth. Increased trust of macrosocial institutions has been accompanied by increased distrust of close relationships. This demutualisation process has led to a change in the nature of social interaction.

Finance, as an intermediary activity, translates individual expectations and promises into monetary units and precise due dates in order to reach an agreement between the parties. Depending on the situation, such an agreement may be more or less formal. The formal cause of finance is thus a quantified expression, which is accepted by the parties, of their mutual commitments and schedules. The combination of quantification of commitments over time and their sometimes highly standardised legal form are the specific components of finance. In this sense, contracts and transactions are the formal cause of finance.

The aforementioned paradox has involved a shift to a more mechanistic, technical way of interacting in which cold, anonymous and often contractual transactions have replaced direct human relationships. Such relationships (sometimes described as 'warm') typify more communitarian societies. The shift from 'relational society' to 'transactional society' thus denotes a change in the nature of social relationships. Finance made this shift easier: relying as it did on institutional trust, it made increased distrust between individuals less of a problem. However, the shift to a contractual, transactional mode has been at the expense of the fiduciary dimension that was a key part of the relational one.

The exemplary cause: pure financial-market theory

Contemporary financial intermediaries are thoroughly familiar with the techniques and tools developed in the wake of the great scientific breakthroughs in the second half of the twentieth century. The scope of what is technically, technologically and scientifically possible can thus be seen as the exemplary cause of the activity carried out by professional intermediaries. In some ways it can be mistaken for what for decades was presented as being politically desirable; for financial euphoria developed against a background of liberalism, which extolled the preeminence and sovereignty of the individual in his life choices.

During the Thirty Euphoric Years, finance – being pure information – was the first sector to benefit from ICT. Finance thus entered the globalisation process very early on, and has since remained its spearhead, leading to the internationalisation of capital flows and actors. Thanks to increasingly swift and effective data transmission and processing, together with reduced unit costs, it is now a sector with a high technological component. To take one example, even if high-frequency trading – which takes place in a matter of milliseconds – remains controversial as regards its added societal value, it is the result of unquestionable technical breakthroughs.

Finance was able to seize the opportunities provided by technological breakthroughs because it was prepared for them by a series of scientific developments that laid the foundations for a new discipline whose formal and quantitative aspects made it seem more like physics than economics: pure theory of market finance. This paradigm opened up a theoretically limitless intellectual field for quantitative manipulations, and information technology provided the necessary tools.

If we are to believe the anecdote, it was Milton Friedman who dubbed this new discipline 'finance'. According to Harry Markowitz, one of the founding fathers of finance, Friedman wondered which field it actually belonged to: statistics (as the large number of statistical series that it used might suggest), economics (given the range of its conclusions) or mathematics (given the tools used). From the mid-1950s onwards, this term 'finance' would spawn the discipline now known as 'market finance', which was to enjoy a meteoric rise. Its apparent level of precision (emphasised by its extreme formalisation), its aesthetics and the prospect of gain that its mastery suggested made it a fascinating and attractive field. It had very little in common with classic finance, now sometimes called 'corporate finance', which is concerned with how non-financial businesses raise funds and use them.

Milton Friedman's brilliant student Harry Markowitz rapidly made a name for himself. Although he did not receive the Nobel Prize until 1991, he is generally considered the father of this new discipline which, in just half a century, has acquired millions of followers and redesigned the business models of financial institutions, and whose logic still presides over the fate of the world economy.

'Market finance' is based on a number of premises that can usefully be summed up here:

- At the heart of the paradigm is the financial manager, whose task and profession are to preserve and expand the idle cash balances that have been entrusted to him, while keeping them in some degree of liquidity. He is not a manager in the classic sense, for he deals with liquid investments rather than entrepreneurial projects. This activity – a derivative one in relation to the real economy – was made possible by the conceptual tools that the theory provides.

- The second component of the paradigm is the notion of risk, which is calculated from historic fluctuations in prices, and then probabilised. The paradigm thus performs an intellectual 'feat' by replacing uncertainty (which by definition cannot be probabilised) with probabilised risk that can hence supposedly be objectivised. The paradigm also closely associates the notion of reward (weighted by risk) with that of risk. The two notions are then used to mark off a two-dimensional space in which each financial asset that is traded on the market can be recorded in terms of its risk/reward characteristics.

- Another key feature of the paradigm is the notion of correlation. This stresses the fact that each asset is affected by the various risk factors in a differentiated manner. It follows that in real life asset prices behave in a more or less correlated manner. This fundamental discovery enables managers to control and manage portfolio risk by covering the risks of some assets with others that have different risk factors. The pursuit of uncorrelated assets has thus become one of the driving forces behind financial innovation.

- The paradigm is centred on the notion of the market – the place where the price of each asset is determined second by second. The price is the cornerstone of the entire intellectual edifice, for without it neither risk nor reward can be calculated. This explains why the paradigm focuses so closely on the need for markets to function smoothly. In order for the market to perform its function of determining prices efficiently, it must be deep, that is, liquid. Liquidity is essential if the interplay of supply and demand is to ensure 'true' prices. The 'efficient market' hypothesis is the intellectual jewel of the paradigm: according to this hypothesis, the market takes account of all the available information when determining prices which, for that very reason are efficient, and in turn, ensure that resources are allocated efficiently.

The efficient cause and the instrumental cause: the financial sector, its products and its functions

At the heart of finance is intermediation between the potential parties in the financial relationship. Interlinkage of the parties' wishes in agreements and contracts is the efficient cause of finance. Today, financial intermediation helps bring these wishes together, much as a sculptor shapes his raw material. Statistically speaking, as we have seen, the importance of finance is reflected by its share of GNP.

The various kinds of contracts, products or services, whether provided for by law or made up ad hoc, are the instruments that intermediaries use to perform their tasks. This set of instruments ensures that the primary users' wishes and actions are operationalised. They are the instrumental cause of finance.

At the same time, the function of the financial sector has changed. In the decades immediately after the Second World War, its function was essential to collect savings and fund private and public investment projects. During the Thirty Euphoric Years, owing to the dematerialisation of money, finance gradually took over almost all payment traffic and, furthermore, became the place where risk was managed. Thus, in addition to its traditional function of allocating capital (collecting savings and funding investment), it now had a new function: allocating risks. According to some assessments, the bulk of the added value generated by finance (in the sense of contribution to GNP) now comes from payment traffic and risk management. In other words, the expansion in the volume of financial activity, measured in terms of its share of GNP, is due to technological breakthroughs and the new intellectual horizons opened up by market finance.

The final cause

Finance emerges at the interface between two kinds of actor: savers, and providers of promises. They do not have a single purpose; each has his own. Convergence and contractualisation are merely the resultant of these two wishes. Finality and purpose carry with them a great deal of ethical questioning; they are important ethical questions.

The aforementioned processes have fundamentally altered the *modus operandi* of finance, as well as its role in the economy and society. The pursuit of financial results, which measures the world in terms of risk and reward, has thus come to predominate well beyond the actual financial sector. It has become part of not only the corporate world, but also the public economy and individuals' lives. Sometimes called financialisation, this process has exposed, and subjected, more and more areas of society to logic of the financial paradigm.

To remain relevant to contemporary finance, ethical thinking must acknowledge the political, social, technological and intellectual specifics of this human activity. This is what is meant by the second update referred to in the introduction to this book. The first will involve opening up finance to ethical concerns and questions – the subject of the next three chapters. First, however, two key notions – ethics and responsibility – must be discussed before moving on to the dilemma: the natural locus of ethical questioning.

2.5 How to define ethics?

What is 'ethics'? Entire libraries have been devoted to the subject. The common thread in these immense efforts down the centuries is the search for reference points and tools to distinguish good from evil when the chips are down. This reflects a typically human – individual as well as social – concern to continue doing the right thing.

To avoid confusion, it is important to distinguish between two levels of ethical research and thinking: fundamental ethics, and applied ethics. Together, these mark out the field of moral philosophy. Thus, upstream of morality (the socially accepted norms that distinguish between good and evil), there is 'fundamental' ethics, which seeks to identify the roots and foundations of moral law. At the other end of this field, where moral law – which by definition is general – crumbles in response to the specific situations that face actors, is 'applied' ethics. In a sense this is an extension of moral law, from which it attempts to derive implications for specific, particular circumstances that differ from one situation to the next. Applied ethics must thus end in action inspired by moral law, without being entirely determined by it – for at the heart of applied ethics is the autonomous, reasoning actor.

The great contemporary philosopher and ethicist, Paul Ricœur (1913–2005), spent much of his life working out a definition of applied ethics. His major work defines ethics as 'the quest/pursuit of an accomplished life – with and for others – in just institutions'.[6] The following comments are made in the light of this definition.

The quoted definition roots ethics in the action of a subject capable of pursuing a goal, that is, of aspiration, as well as will guided by the search for coherence. Pursuit or quest of a goal is more than a whim or a passing desire – it implies a degree of determination over time and perseverance in effort. We can speak of reasoned, conscious effort that can lead to choices and hence sacrifices. Ricœur therefore places the search for meaning (in French, *sens*) at the heart of ethical action. The French word *sens* can be interpreted in two ways: meaning and direction. This is perfectly suited to the present argument. It refers to both reason, which must be used in each situation, and coherence, which requires us to move beyond the isolated act. The role of ethics is then to ensure coherence between isolated situations and life as a whole. Thus, in combination, meaning and direction are what determine the quest/pursuit of an 'accomplished life'.[7]

What is an accomplished life? As defined by Ricœur, it is like north on the ethical compass. It is here that the pursuit of development of human nature, the best use of our talents and personal aptitudes, the perfecting of our virtues and indeed our response to an inner vocation or call come together, without forgetting the material conditions for existence. Ricœur does not call for an overall response, but encourages us all to consider our own definitions and conditions for an accomplished life. Thus, he says, the subject's first responsibility is in relation to his 'ego' and pursuit of an accomplished life, including its material dimension. This 'ego' has nothing in common with the 'economic man' (*homo oeconomicus*) of economic theory, who is thoroughly selfish and materialistic. Here, as the rest of Ricœur's definition makes clear, this 'ego' is open and concerned about others. The Ricœurian definition thus has two dimensions: the immaterial metric of values, and the metric of the impact and consequences of the act on the individual involved and beyond.

In the rest of his definition, Ricœur takes good care to add two more conditions. These remind us that, beyond the actual subject, the pursuit/quest of an accomplished life involves and affects the group, thus limiting the sovereignty of the 'ego' and requiring it to take account of others. To deserve the description 'accomplished' in the ethical sense, all human existence must – to Ricœur this is a non-negotiable condition – take account of others, live 'with and for others'. The two propositions designate (a) the harmony of existence within a group and the non-conflictual nature of relationships and (b) the service and reciprocity dimension. The second metric of ethics is thus provided by the impact of the subject's decisions and acts on others. Who the term 'others' includes remains an open question. We will return to this when discussing the notion of responsibility.

Ricœur's definition also refers to just institutions as a natural horizon of ethics. The pursuit of an accomplished life aims not only to benefit from just institutions, but also to strengthen and consolidate them. Let us assume that Ricœur is using the term 'institution' in the broad sense, including both formal and informal institutions, laws, habits and customs. The definition then highlights the dialectic between each act and the institutions that exist in society. Every act performed with concern for ethics thus helps, marginally and infinitesimally, to consolidate the justice and justness of institutions in society, while allowing them to evolve and adapt to new challenges. Just as coral reefs are constantly built and altered by billions of microorganisms, just institutions are the resultant of billions of microdecisions inspired by the pursuit of ethics. Conversely, acts performed without concern for others and the 'pursuit of an accomplished life' are a threat to just institutions, for they may cause collateral damage that is unrelated to the act itself. Respect for the 'spirit of just laws' is therefore the third metric of ethics.

In conclusion, says Ricœur, the pursuit of an accomplished life is not just a 'private' matter – it is not socially neutral, for it affects not only the actual subject but also the immediate group, and society as a whole. In barely fifteen words, his definition captures the essentials of the relationship between individual aspirations, relations with others as people, and social harmony, that is, institutions. It thus focuses on everyone's responsibility not only in progressing towards the accomplished life, but also in contributing to social harmony and the common good.

The multidimensional nature of Ricœur's definition makes it attractive to non-specialists, for it helps us deal with a number of contrasts that have divided ethical thinkers for centuries. The first of these is the classic contrast between the ethics of virtue (Aristotle, Thomas Aquinas) and the ethics of duty (Kant and Jonas). Both appear in Ricœur's definition: the ethics of virtue in the appeal for the accomplished life which must be built up by effort and constancy, and the ethics of duty in the confrontation between acts and just institutions. The second contrast corresponds to Max Weber's distinction[8] between the ethics of conviction and the ethics of responsibility. Whereas the former resembles the ethics of virtue, the latter refers to the impact that acts may have on others, particularly those for whom the subject is responsible. Here again, Ricœur manages to integrate the essentials of the two approaches. The former (conviction) is part of the pursuit of the accomplished life; the second (responsibility) entails concern for others, as we will see below.

2.6 Responsibility

The notion of responsibility is a key aspect of contemporary debates on ethics. Ethics and responsibility are in many ways similar, as we can see from Weber's reference to the ethics of responsibility. However, they differ as regards the importance of the legal dimension – a key part of the notion of responsibility.

Two situations must be distinguished when it comes to responsibility: responsibility assumed when the action is performed (responsible action) and responsibility assigned after the event (ex-post responsibility).[9]

In the case of 'responsible action', the actor assumes responsibility – for example, the responsibility that goes with his post – and will act to the best of his ability in order to meet people's expectations. Acting responsibly means taking account of the potential consequences and impact of one's acts within the scope of responsibility. Thus, in their daily acts, parents assume responsibility for their families, team leaders do so for their colleagues, and so on. The responsibility they assume goes together with (a) a clear view of the purposes of the action and the values that command it, and (b) awareness of the impact these acts will have on others. Calls for responsible consumption or investment thus stigmatise the effects of certain daily acts and the relationship between them and defended values. Responsible action is thus action that is aware of the consequences to others and the values involved. Ethics in the sense of concern for others and responsible action is thus one and the same thing.

Ex-post responsibility is responsibility that is assigned after the event, once the often adverse consequences of an act have become apparent. The ethical reading of such responsibility usually has three dimensions: the actor's intention; the actor's awareness of the potential consequences; and the extent of the damage. As for the legal reading, this mainly focuses on the legal aspects. In legal practice, ex-ante responsibility does not coincide with ex-post responsibility, as regards either the subject or the damage.

Whereas the actor's intention and awareness of the consequences are part of the responsible action discussed above, the question of damage is part of ex-post responsibility. At this stage lawyers take over, in two different areas: punishing the actor, and repairing the damage. The question of punishment is an eminently legal one, for it involves the government and the law. Repairing the damage, on the other hand, may also have an ethical dimension, for the nature of the repair will differ according to whether or not the damage is reversible. It is reversible if it can be repaired quickly and completely, for instance when stolen goods are recovered and returned to their owner without damage or loss within a reasonable period of time. However, if it is not immediately reversible, the question of (usually monetary) compensation arises, with endless arguments about the nature of the damage and how to assess it. The annals of economic and financial lawsuits, such as the BP trial following the Gulf of Mexico disaster, are highly instructive in this regard.

All responsibility relationships (whether ex-post or ex-ante) are basically relationships between (a) the subject acting with a margin of freedom of action and (b) the instances he must answer to for his actions. It is the way in which the relationship between the subject and the instances is organised that determines the extent to which law and ethics match.

Depending on whether subjects are individuals, legal persons (institutions) or individuals acting on behalf of a legal person, they must answer to different instances, or according to different processes. Whereas institutions' ex-post responsibility is purely legal, individuals' responsibility may also be ethical or moral. This means that an institution's legal responsibility does not relieve individuals acting on their behalf of their ethical responsibility.[10] As for ex-ante responsibility, the jury is still out on the issue of whether institutions have a conscience or are capable of committing moral errors.[11]

As for the instances to which subjects must answer for their actions, one can envisage three kinds of situations (which are not mutually exclusive): their conscience (which brings us back to the ethics of virtue and Ricœur's accomplished life), their direct or indirect clients (the group, and Ricœur's 'others') and the community (just institutions and the common good). Among these three authorities, only the relationship between subjects and their clients may be part of the regulatory and institutional framework that is external to the actor, whereas both conscience and concern for the common good are rooted in subjects' own characteristics and dependent on their predispositions.

The relationship between subjects and the authorities they are expected to answer to may take two different forms: either it is experienced by subjects from within, or it is imposed from without. Although, as with ethics, responsibility experienced from within permeates every act involving subjects' freedom, responsibility from without only intervenes – in the form of punishment or a request for financial compensation – when damage has occurred. Such outside intervention may involve an awareness that will henceforth induce subjects to experience their ex-ante responsibility and any ex-post guilt more fully; for the ex-ante responsibility relationship is not fixed, and may expand and be deepened as subjects progress ethically.

In conclusion, the notion of responsibility, apart from its own legal dimension, leads ethical analysis to look more closely at the scope of possible consequences. At the theoretical level, the field of possible impacts of an action expands as scientific knowledge increases. The extreme example is provided by the famous 'butterfly effect'; this reveals an infinite chain of causalities and probabilities which, thanks to catastrophe theory, links the beating of a butterfly's wings to a tornado thousands of kilometres away. However, at the practical level, only the most immediate, second-order consequences can be apprehended and hence are ethically relevant.

Without a margin of freedom of choice, there can be no ethical behaviour or ex-ante responsibilities. The 'dilemma' is then the locus where ethics takes place or responsibility can be assumed.

2.7 The dilemma: the locus of ethics

If the actor were utterly determined, both mentally and physically, the question of pursued goals, just institutions or responsibility would not even occur to him. However, if it does cross his mind, it is because he is aware of his room for manoeuvre, however small, and intends to use it in the name of ethics and responsibility for his acts.[12]

All economic and financial decisions concern the distribution of wealth and resources in time and space between the protagonists and, in some cases, third parties. They hence all relate to what is usually termed 'commutative justice'. This considers what everyone should be entitled to in moral law. The conditions of the transaction are therefore the natural locus for ethical questions. What is the 'right' price – not the best price for one of the parties, but the one in keeping with the assumed responsibilities and ethics? The answer given by contemporary economics, which rejects the ethical dimension, is that the 'market price' is by definition 'right' – whereas what has long concerned classic moralists is the question of the *justum pretium* (just or fair price).

Without going to extremes, the ethical question thus only arises when the subject is aware that there is a choice, and when he wishes to make that choice in the name of an accomplished life and/or concern for justice. These two conditions rule out situations in which conscience or perspicacity are dulled, or in which the subject lacks the will and, in some cases, the courage to act. Such questions confront the actor with a dilemma: what to do, and why?[13]

Such situations are common in the financial sector, where choices are often presented and analysed in purely technical terms, such as the aforementioned market price. This helps to conceal the ethical dimension by focusing on issues of constrained maximisation or optimisation. Perseverance and courage are then needed to take risks and discover the underlying ethical dimension.

Every day we perform a large number of acts, but relatively few of them involve ethical dilemmas or are based on truly well-considered decisions. We act in response to automatic reflexes or habits acquired earlier. Only situations that are new, or seen from a new angle, trigger a true decision-making process that leads us to discover the range of possibilities, envisage the consequences and identify the values and priorities that are involved. These dilemmas result in actions that pave the way for many future acts. Such 'structuring moments or decisions'[14] need to be recognised and approached with due consideration. They are dilemmas in which the ethical dimension and questions of responsibility come to the fore, for the decisions in question often have major implications for ourselves, those we are responsible for, and the broader environment.

The relationship between automatic reflexes and dilemmas varies not only from person to person, but also in the light of a person's experience and ethical baggage. We should not confuse habits and automatic reflexes with 'habitus'. Habitus is a 'good habit', one forged by a deliberate effort to comply with ethical standards. The notion of habitus is often used in connection with ethics of virtue: education in virtue involves practice, which with time becomes habitus – the habit of doing the right thing.[15]

Thus, the more an actor has acquired a habitus of ethical behaviour and judgement, the fewer dilemmas he will encounter, unlike a beginner confronted with the same situations. Yet this does not mean that dilemmas will disappear forever; they may occur, or recur, in a new situation or a familiar one presented in a new light that reveals hitherto unknown aspects. In such cases, the actor's habitus, instinct or intuition will be unable to cope. He will have to return to reasoning, identify the dilemma, envisage the alternatives and their consequences and ethical qualities before deciding and acting.

It follows that the dilemma, possibly later solved with the help of an habitus, is the primary locus for ethics and responsibility. Every actor concerned by the implications for others of the choices available to him will have to analyse the situation, envisage the alternatives and their many possible consequences, and weigh them up in terms of his pursuit of an accomplished life and his concern for justice.

If the acting subject is a person, the conditions for ethical questioning will be based on personal attitudes and capabilities. This is not the case if the actor is a group: a committee, a board, a business, a parliament or some other regulatory body. In that case, actions and decisions are collective not only in their implications but also in the way they come about. Account must therefore be taken of an additional condition: minimum agreement between the members of the body on the conditions for an ethical choice. In many cases there is no such agreement, especially when the technical dimension conceals the ethical implications and the actors make no attempt to consider them. Such situations impose even more radical choices on minority groups. The only alternatives they often have 'shut up or exit',[16] for collective decision-making tends to encourage deadlock on 'soft' issues, that is ones that cannot be grasped in quantitative terms, unless the specific corporate culture has made such concerns an integral part of its everyday practice.

2.8 The four dimensions of an ethical assessment

As we have just seen, the dilemma is a situation in which several actions are envisaged and compared. Whereas identifying possibilities depends on a close knowledge of the situation and an ability to imagine alternatives, comparison may rely on a more general method.

Inspired by Ricœur's definitions and the foregoing considerations on responsibility, the work of the Observatoire de la Finance has resulted in a list of four concerns to be taken into account when the alternatives for economic and financial action are assessed in ethical terms:[17]

- *Concern for the actor's own economic performance.* The 'accomplished life' also has a material dimension, which is the very reason for all economic and financial activity. Positive fall-out is therefore the sufficient and necessary condition for envisaging action, and must be assessed first. Fall-out for the entity is measured here– the business or public body – rather than for the person who makes the decision within it.

- *Concern for rules and principles.* This covers Ricœur's 'just institutions' in the formal sense, for it enables us to make clear to what extent the envisaged action will strengthen or weaken the existing institutional order both outside and within the business.
- *Concern for the intristic quality of the act.* This situates the intristic qualities of the act on the individual decision-maker's scale of values, and may concern not only the ethical but also the professional qualities of the envisaged act. This concern reflects the actor's 'conviction' and responsibility for a set of knowledge and techniques that he possesses through his work or training.
- *Concern for impact on third parties.* This assesses the impact on 'others', those who will be affected by the consequences outside the narrow group of those directly affected by the decision. Jean-Loup Dherse[18]

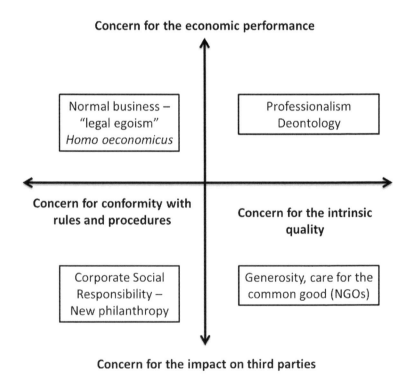

Figure 2.1 Mind the Gap assessment method © Observatoire de la Finance

liked to say that ethics in decision-making involves taking account of the impact 'on those who cannot reward or punish the decision-maker', that is those who have no say in the matter. The 'third party' here is the passive, voiceless third party – not the consumer of a product whose quality could be altered, or the employee whose salary will be raised. Concern for impact involves taking account of the periphery of the decision.

A graphic of these four concerns is the backbone of the 'Mind the Gap' assessment method devised by the Observatoire de la Finance and used to tackle ethical dilemmas as well as assess the presence and importance of ethical considerations in corporate cultures.

The next three chapters will extend the above ethical thinking to the field of contemporary finance. The saver, the creditor – who offers credit – and the *rentier* (who lives on his unearned income) are the points of reference for the dilemmas discussed in the first of these chapters. In the second, the dilemmas analysed are those facing fund users: debtors in the case of consumer loans, and public bodies and businesses that obtain finance. Finally, the third will look at the financial operator, the intermediary. Conflicts of interest, the internal organisation of institutions, the problem of market integrity and those of supervision and regulation will all be discussed.

Notes

1 Pierre-Noël Giraud, *Le commerce des promesses: petit traité sur la finance moderne*, Denoël, Paris, 2001.
2 The dollar is a unique case. Although technically a fiduciary currency that depends on the survival of the American economy, it is unreservedly accepted around the world because of unshakable faith in that economy's global power. This creates major advantages for the American economy, whose 'signature' is worth money.
3 Friedrich Hayek, *Denationalisation of Money*, Institute for International Affairs, London, 1976; 'Toward Free Market Money', *Wall Street Journal*, 19 August 1977.
4 Credit cards and modern electronic payment instruments are a blend of the public means of payment and its private vehicle, which are effectively inseparable. Payment then takes place in 'Mastercard euros, pound or dollars', whose effective value exceeds the value of public money by the amount of the commission charged. Mastercard claims include an element of credit risk that is not found in hard cash.
5 Théodore de Régnon, *La métaphysique des causes d'après Saint Thomas et Albert le Grand*, Victor Retaux Éditeur, Paris, 1906; Jonathan Lear, *Aristotle: the desire to understand*, Cambridge University Press, 1997.
6 Paul Ricœur, *Soi-même comme un autre*, Le Seuil, Paris, 1990, p. 202.
7 Hugues Puel, *Une éthique pour l'économie: ethos, crises, choix*, Le Cerf, Collection Recherches morales, Paris, 2010.

8 'We must be clear about the fact that all ethically oriented conduct may be guided by one of two fundamentally differing and irreconcilably opposed maxims: conduct can be oriented to an "ethic of ultimate ends" or to an "ethic of responsibility". This is not to say that an ethic of ultimate ends is identical with irresponsibility, or that an ethic of responsibility is identical with unprincipled opportunism. Naturally nobody says that. However, there is an abysmal contrast between conduct that follows the maxim of an ethic of ultimate ends – that is, in religious terms, "The Christian does rightly and leaves the results with the Lord" – and conduct that follows the maxim of an ethic of responsibility, in which case one has to give an account of the foreseeable results of one's action' (Weber, M. 'Politics as a Vocation'. In *From Max Weber: Essays in Sociology* (pp. 77–128), ed. and trans. H. H. Gerth and C. Wright Mills, New York: Oxford University Press, 1946).

9 Roman Ingarden, *Über die Verantwortung: ihre ontischen Fundamente*, Stuttgart, Reclam, 1970; Bénédict Winiger, *Verantwortung, Reversibilität und Verschulden*, Mohr Siebeck, Tübingen, 2013.

10 The Sarbanes-Oxley Act was adopted in 2002 after the Enron scandal, mainly in order to confront the directors of listed American companies with their personal responsibility. It requires them to personally certify the integrity of their accounts, failing which they are subject to hefty individual penalties.

11 Kenneth Goodpaster, *Conscience and Corporate Culture*, Wiley-Blackwell, Oxford, 2007, and Justin Welby, *Can Companies Sin? 'Whether', 'How' and 'Who' in Company Accountability,* Grove Books Ltd, Cambridge, 1992.

12 Repeated testimony by people who have experienced the worst horrors of the twentieth century suggests that anyone truly wishing to pursue an accomplished life will find the tiniest margins of freedom for mental or material action regardless of their circumstances, however inhuman or terrifying these may be. It is only when people are subjected to mental manipulation that their consciences may be blunted – as in the case of brainwashing, conditioning or other dehumanising acts that are deliberately designed to destroy their inner structure.

13 Étienne Perrot, *L'art de décider en situations complexes*, Desclée de Brouwer, Paris 2007; *Le discernement managérial*, Desclée de Brouwer, Paris, 2012.

14 Joseph Badaracco speaks of 'defining moments': see Badaracco, Joseph L. J., *Defining Moments: When Managers Must Choose between Right and Right*, Harvard Business School Press, Boston, 1997.

15 Ulrich Hemel, Andreas Fitzsche and Jürgen Manemann (eds), *Habituelle Unternehmensethik: von der Ethik zum Ethos*, Nomos, Baden-Baden, 2012.

16 Albert Hirschman, *Exit, Voice and Loyalty: Response to Decline in Firms, Organizations and States*, Harvard University Press, Cambridge MA, 1970.

17 For more information, see www.obsfin.ch.

18 Co-author with Hugues Minguet of *L'Éthique ou le Chaos?*, Presses de la Renaissance, Paris, 1999.

3 The fund holder's ethical dilemmas

Savers and *rentiers*

In order for finance to work, there must be payment in return for promises. In the absence of liquidity and temporarily idle cash balances, there can be no finance. This chapter will focus on the final fund holder, the person that accumulates the funds, invests them perhaps in the expectation of reusing them, and hopes to earn income from them. The ethical dilemmas and questions that may face savers, speculators or *rentiers* will be discussed in the following pages.

The action of the individual saver is today extended by his specialised agents: asset managers, pension funds or life insurers. These are institutions and businesses acting on the saver's or *rentier*'s behalf. They also encounter ethical questions, which will be discussed below. The macroeconomic question of institutional arrangements and regulations on the place of savings and private income in society will also be considered.

3.1 From non-consumption to savings

To begin with, it is important to mention that the question of property and responsibility for it is one of the main issues on which moral traditions have focused. Contemporary law largely avoids this issue by establishing the concept of a sovereign owner who is free to use – and misuse – his property as he sees fit. Yet this does not dispose of the potential question raised by moral law regarding the free use of property. Especially in the Catholic tradition, property is merely a deposit to be managed for the greater good of all. This means that the use of property is constrained from the outset by concern for others.

Non-consumption of immediately disposable income may occur in two typical situations. In the great majority of cases it involves self-sacrifice in order to attain an important future goal. Here again, we must distinguish savings and deliberate self-sacrifice from forced savings as a result of legal requirements or long-term contractual commitments, such as pension funds

or life insurance contributions. In less frequent cases, which are nevertheless significant in terms of their volume, non-consumption is the result of
technical or physical inability to consume all one's income. There is clearly
very little in common between the colossal fortunes (savings) of industrial
dynasties managed by 'family offices', often over several generations, and
individuals that build up a family fortune by making daily sacrifices. In the
former case, the moment in time when the savings will have to be used for
other purposes is both vague and very remote, whereas in the latter case the
moment of dissaving is predictable (a new car, retirement, holidays). This is
a key difference that affects the way in which people save.

The first ethical question raised by non-consumption and savings is thus
what purpose they serve. There are three possible answers, each with major
ethical implications:

- The first focuses on austerity and frugality of consumption and, more
  broadly, way of life. Regardless of the level of income, consumption is
  geared to essential needs. Savings are not a goal in themselves – they
  are, at most, what is left over. There are then two possible situations:
  the remaining income is used differently or saved, or else it is simply
  abandoned without any expectation of return. An austere way of life
  and savings – with almost automatic accumulation of assets – have
  traditionally been associated with Protestantism. As for donation or
  sharing of what is left over, these are widely practised. Appeals to share
  what is left over are among the major arguments for fair, ethical or
  responsible savings and investment.
- The second possible justification for savings is the prospect of a future
  need or acquisition. A car, a home or retirement are all good reasons
  to save. Future use is thus part of the motivation for the present act
  of non-consumption. Such savings involve intertemporal transfer of
  resources: today's self-sacrifice is the preliminary to tomorrow's satisfaction. The saver's goal is to 'secure' purchasing power and ensure a
  reasonable income.
- The third reason to save is the wish, which involves self-sacrifice,
  to create assets that can be passed on to future generations or, more
  prosaically, to get rich and one day become a *rentier*. The *rentier* is a
  stock figure in nineteenth-century literature (especially the works of
  Emile Zola), living on interest and other income paid to him by those,
  including the government, to whom he has previously lent money.
  The extreme case of the saver is the miser, who seeks to possess
  liquidity that gives him power and control over others. This situation
  will be discussed below.

Frugality focuses on the present, whereas in the other two cases the motive for savings is geared to the future. However, the question of intertemporal preference is not ethically neutral. Is the accomplished life built up in the present, or is it designed entirely with a view to the future? The timescale of human life, and material responsibility towards future generations, are questions that are frequently raised in the main cultures and religions. They are by no means specific to the modern era; but today they are raised in new contexts because of the highly specialised financial products that operators do not hesitate to offer savers.

Logically, the choice of which financial product to use should be based on the fund holder's notion of why he is saving. However, in today's increasingly aggressive marketing and consultancy practices, the question of purpose tends to be pre-empted by the choice of the financial product proposed by the seller. It is therefore up to the fund holder to find the means and the time to consider what his savings mean and what part they should play in his view of the 'accomplished life'. This is the key ethical question.

3.2 Intergenerational assets

'Intergenerational assets' are material wealth that can be passed on within families from one generation to the next. The notion of continuity – with ethical implications – is based on acknowledgement of intergenerational rights and obligations. In some cultures, particularly in Africa (but also among the Iroquois), intergenerational ethics requires account to be taken of interests extending over seven generations: three in the past, one in the present and three in the future. Except as regards succession, this dimension is completely disregarded by present-day law; instead, the generation that currently holds the funds has rights and no duties. To compensate in part for this, account must be taken of intergenerational ethical requirements.[1]

Today, as statistically measured in Western countries, households' assets consist of three main components: the family dwelling, family businesses, and financial savings in the sense of holding of financial assets. Each of these is capable of absorbing the savings flow, and hence of growing. Although the first two have a direct material counterpart, they may also have a financial dimension (particularly in the form of loans), but this is only temporary. As for the third component, it is entirely financial.

Savers who intend to build up assets are thus at a crossroads. They may opt either to acquire financial assets, or to make use of home savings schemes, or to build up business assets by not distributing profits, or to make liquidity available to relatives (children, parents) to help them buy a home or set up a business.

Why choose which option? At least four considerations will interact in ways specific to each saver, and these are subject to constant variations. Each of them has an ethical dimension.

- First of all, necessity or, more specifically, existential choices. These include purchasing a dwelling (other than for speculative purposes) or deciding to set up an independent business. In both cases, savings go straight into the real world without financial assets being involved.
- Second, the relative profitability of the various savings instruments. From mere savings accounts to sophisticated deposit accounts, the spectrum is almost infinite, extending to joint investment funds and other instruments devised by financial engineering. There is a shift from products with guaranteed rewards and returns to products with usually higher rates of reward but higher levels of risk. This is where the third component of the decision comes in: the nature and the level of risk acceptable to the various savers.
- A saver who knows that his essential needs will be covered in the medium term is more able to take risks that one who, for instance, is saving to send his children to university in ten years' time. In the former case the main motive for saving is financial return; in the latter, on the contrary, it is security. Between these two extremes, the question of purposes arises again. Ethical thinking enables the acceptable level and nature of risk to be determined. The further the chosen instrument is removed from what is specific and directly controllable, the more abstract the links of trust, and the associated risks, become.
- The fourth consideration adds another dimension to the classic risk/reward discourse and questions the specific use of savings. The saver thus asks himself what 'purpose' his savings will serve, and what impact his wealth will have on other people's lives. Savers with free liquidity who follow Ricœur's injunction to take account of others explicitly consider that this belongs to their area of responsibility. Although they do not intend to give their funds away, they do seek to make them useful. This involves not only the saver's values, but also his tolerance for abstract answers. For some people, it will be enough to know that their savings have gone into a 'responsible or ethical fund'; but others will want to know more about the end user of their funds and the way he employs them. This consideration is ultimately linked to the previous two: what additional risks, what reductions in rewards or what losses is the saver prepared to accept in order to abide by his values and convictions?

The case of 'sustainable finance' discussed below is an opportunity to deepen the whereabouts of the implementation in real life of the societal responsibility of the saver.

3.3 Implementing the societal responsibility of the saver: 'sustainable finance'

'Sustainable finance' is a growing segment of financial products and advisory services which aim at building awareness of the ultimate owner of funds of the extra-financial impacts that derive form the activity of agents in which the ultimate owner is invested. 'Sustainable finance' shares this concern with other lines of products and services known under such names as 'ethical finance', 'solidarity finance' or 'responsible finance'. All these efforts have in common the integration of extra-financial data into the financial decision process. As such all these initiatives carry a strong message in terms of the ex-ante responsibility of the ultimate saver and/or of his agent. Indeed they extend the perimeter of responsibility of the asset holder beyond the financial performance to include direct and indirect impacts of the related enterprises on environment and society.[2]

As market enterprises, the providers of 'sustainable' products and services propose to savers tools which include in their assets' assessments the social and environmental impacts. The underlying and fundamental conviction of these activities rests on a strong premise according to which financial performance converges with social and environmental benefits, at least in the long run. This act of faith is supposed to make the savers choice easy as the situation is expected to be a 'win-win' one. This being said, and despite many efforts to substantiate empirically this convictions, the results of research are highly dispersed. Some studies conclude that convergence exists, other are inconclusive while still others stress divergence between financial and extra-financial performance. Studies at hand are deeply heterogeneous regarding at least four dimensions: the matrix used to define what is defined as sustainable; the matrix used to measure the financial performance, especially the choice of the benchmark; the period under study; and finally the markets under review.

In consequence, because of not fully conclusive empirical evidence, the saver who is sensitive to extra-financial impacts has no certainty as to the mutual relationship between the two orders of performance. He/she must then not only consider the promised 'win-win' situation where 'doing well' goes hand in hand with 'doing good', but also situations of divergence – that is, those situations where the commitment to sustainability has a cost in terms of risk and return profile of the portfolio. This is true anyhow, as a 'sustainable' investor will either exclude or under-weight certain components of the investment universe. By doing so he/she loses some of the advantages of diversification and thus increases investment risk. The 'best in class' investment strategy, may significantly reduce the sectoral diversification bias.

Sustainable finance is today fashionable and may look attractive and promising to many but this requires at least four qualifications.

- 'Sustainable finance' encompasses today a wide variety of definitions and methods of measurement of extra-financial impacts. In consequence the assessment of the same financial assets in terms of its sustainability may vary from one methodology to another.
- Whatever the used methodology is, the assessment of extra-financial impact is constrained by scarcity of corresponding data. Financial statements of enterprises have to comply with clear requirements and accounting norms. This is not the case with when it comes to extra-financial reporting. Enterprises communicate selectively on these issues despite the efforts of initiatives such as 'Triple Bottom Line' or 'Global Reporting Initiative' which aim at establishing a uniform and strict reporting format. In this situation, sustainability experts have to rely on a wide spectrum of secondary data sources. This limits the quality of the analysis and increases its cost.
- By building savers' awareness of the consequences of his financial decisions, sustainable finance also aims at creating a virtuous loop between the saver and those of the enterprises which take their social responsibility seriously. These enterprises can expect to be compensated for their societal efforts by being chosen by sustainable investors. In consequence of this additional demand, their share prices should raise and their cost of capital fall. Such a virtuous loop will ultimately bring to life the 'win-win' scenario referred to above.
- Finally, sustainable finance also targets the not-yet sustainable enterprises as some of its initiatives develop 'shareholder activism' which seeks a direct interaction with the enterprise either at general assemblies or more directly via interaction with the management. By doing this, shareholder activists seek either to convince the enterprises to align their practices on the preferences of 'sustainable' investors or to constrain them to do so under the threat of a scandal or boycott of their products.

In spite of all the imperfections related to the underlying definitions and methodologies, sustainable finance has the merit of reminding the saver of the question about the true meaning and impact of his savings. In itself this is salutary as the question meaning tends to be marginalised in the general rush for performance. In some countries, public authorities extend this question to pension funds and require them to explain their stance on sustainability in their financial statements. Such a legal requirement has to be considered in the light of the primary mandate that these institutions have received form their members, especially on the question related to the possible cost or losses in financial performance that may occur as a consequence of sustainability preferences. This debate will last for a long time.

3.4 Forced savings: life insurance and pension funds

The second half of the twentieth century saw the spread of financial products – and the associated institutions – that enabled savers to assign their savings to specific events such as death, invalidity or retirement. In some countries, insurance of all or part of these risks was made compulsory. This situation has two potential consequences. It extends insurance of some risks to the whole population, but at the same time denies households free access to part of their income. This explains why the part of savings automatically assigned to compulsory payments is sometimes known as 'forced savings'. The second consequence of compulsory insurance of some risks is that it limits situations in which people may become dependent on government assistance when the time comes for them to retire. Although compulsory contributions restrict freedom of access to one's income, they also reduce the amount of 'free-riding' in social policy by forcing everyone to save, including those who would be most likely to squander their income. The issues of social ethics associated with the spread of social security schemes will be discussed later on.

In addition to compulsory savings, average savers can sign long-term savings or insurance contracts such as life-insurance or pension policies. The principle behind such institutions is to guarantee over the long term the payment of either a lump sum or a lifetime annuity. Life insurance also covers the risk of early death, ensuring that an agreed amount is paid to a survivor. In ethical terms, the use of such instruments allows savers to take account of relatives who might by left in financial difficulties by an early death, but at the same time it structurally deprives the household of part of its income. This again raises the ethical issue of which risks should be accepted by the household and which should be covered by financial promises of an insurer.

Pressure to individualise our lives, referred to earlier as 'demutualisation', may induce some people to protect themselves rather than run the risk of depending on their relatives in the future. This reflects a distrust of future generations, and a preference of the elderly for formal promises by insurers to implicit promises by descendants, in which they above all see a risk of dependence. In doing so, however, they are using up assets that would otherwise have been passed on to future generations. This creates an ethical dilemma.

3.5 Interest: the (forbidden) fruit of savings

Savers make their assets temporarily available to others in return not only for a promise that the sum will be repaid on an agreed date, but also for remuneration – in other words, interest.

Interest on loans is the most controversial financial practice in the three Abrahamic religions: Judaism, Christianity and Islam. Without going further into the various arguments, what they agree on is that lending with interest is a morally questionable practice because it imposes a burden on the debtor and exposes him to risks that are not symmetrical with the benefits accruing to the creditor. The latter enjoys a twofold guarantee of being reimbursed and being remunerated, whereas the debtor has no certainty as to how things will turn out, for no one is safe from sudden reversals of fortune. In other words, the debtor guarantees the creditor a future over which he has no control. It is this unfair distribution of risks that has led to the prohibition on lending with interest, particularly in Islam. Judaism also prohibits it within the Jewish community, but does allow it in relations with non-Jews.

The question of the legitimacy of lending with interest and the resulting income has also been the subject of much debate within Christianity.[3] Three arguments from this debate (which cannot be summed up here) may be mentioned at this point:

- Anyone who takes an active part in the economy has the primary task of producing new wealth by working and by making full use of his resources. Diverting resources into interest-bearing loans would deflect them from this primary task of creating wealth. The only exception is lending in cases of distress, to help those in need. Then, and only then, are lending and its remuneration justified, but not in the form of interest. The remuneration makes up for loss of income that the lender would have earned if he had used the lent sum in his own work. This argument thus leads to a ban on money-related professions, rather than lending as such.[4]
- The second argument concerns the morally unacceptable nature of the creditor's intervention in the debtor's daily life by making him pay interest. This is supposedly tantamount to theft. This argument – which was developed long before the industrial revolution and business loans, and hence referred solely to lending in cases of distress – lost much

of its force with the development of commercial and business loans. The famous distinction made by Jean Calvin in 1548 thus confirmed a practice that was already fairly widespread and tolerated: he utterly condemned interest on loans in case of distress, but allowed it for business loans, on the grounds that the lender was morally entitled to part of the profit from the project being financed. Two centuries later, the Vatican lifted the official ban on interest-bearing loans, but did not actually authorise them. It was everyone's duty to assess the particular circumstances of each transaction, especially the distribution of risk that burdened the debtor.

- The third aspect concerns the amount of coercion that may be used if the debtor fails to meet his commitments. In ancient cultures, it was accepted that he could be imprisoned or even enslaved. This highlights the problem of distribution of risk: whereas the lender was risking some money, the borrower was risking his personal freedom, and that of his family. Two limits gradually emerged. The first was a collective one: the Jewish tradition of the Jubilee. According to Leviticus, all debts would be automatically cancelled – reset to zero – in every fiftieth year. The second was an individual one: there were situations in which the lender could not be reimbursed if this would leave the debtor destitute.

A *rentier* is someone who lives on his unearned income. This raises two ethical problems. The first of these has just been mentioned: whether lending and interest are legitimate as such. The second is that the *rentier* not only protects his income against risk, but thus avoids the material constraint – whose importance is stressed in some traditions – of having to work, that is also produce wealth for others. This is not a new argument, for it has always been used to vilify the idle – parasitic – classes.

During the Thirty Euphoric Years, financial techniques seemed to bring the prospect of living without working within reach. Numerous financial products and insurance policies were built up on (false) certainties about infinitely guaranteed rewards. The change in the financial landscape since 2007 is now undermining most of these products and institutions. The myth of 'never having to work again' now seems less realistic to current generations than it did to the baby-boomers born in the 1950s. However, this does not eliminate the ethical problem raised by an idle, self-centred life of indifference to others, even if such benefits are perfectly legal.[5]

3.6 Gambling or financing?

The aforementioned dilemmas associated with savings disregard the motivation of purely and simply accumulating monetary wealth – for money exerts a seductive force that ethical thinking cannot afford to ignore. The power promised by the possession of the 'general equivalent' has always been intoxicating, but it has now reached its peak, for the society around us is a 'market society'. Money is supposedly the key to happiness, for it allows us to do without our fellows. Everything can be bought – not just goods and services, but also other people. Just institutions, moral values and people without a voice in society are then pushed aside. The question of how to make money has been with us throughout history. As with Midas, or the figure of the miser, the idea is not to use it but to possess it. Desire for money is the whole aim. When society was governed by moral laws, greed and avarice were vices that were practised in dark corners, often with a sense of guilt. This all changed with the advent of financialisation, during the Thirty Euphoric Years, for the myth of the efficient market was based on the idea that selfishness would lead to the social optimum.

The late-1980s cult film reflected this change in mentality. At a shareholders' meeting the 'hero' Gordon Gekko (played by Michael Douglas) shouts 'Greed is good', to thunderous applause. This now emblematic scene shows that market-efficiency propaganda had turned greed and love of gain into social virtues. The headlong pursuit of greater assets, with no justification other than more-more-more, had begun. The classic ethical question of self-denial 'How much is too much?' was henceforth dismissed. Although in some traditions wealth is perceived as a sign of divine blessing, none of them advocates the headlong pursuit of monetary accumulation.[6]

'How much is too much?' is an eminently ethical question. There are at least two dimensions to this dilemma: other people, particularly partners in the financial relationship, who are often ignored, and the resources used to keep multiplying assets. This raises two issues.

Savers can choose between two main groups of financial products: debts (bonds, bank deposits, and so on) and shares in listed businesses. Loans (including bonds) involve contributing directly to the funding of an activity, whereas buying shares on a market does not. The business is not directly affected by the purchase of its shares, but only indirectly through the share price, which the purchase may well have helped to sustain. Savers who buy shares thus gamble on the future performance of their prices. If they buy today, they probably do so with the intention of reselling at a profit in due course.

Shares were traditionally held for years at a time; but in recent decades this period has greatly decreased, and is nowadays counted (on average) in months or even days. The ethical question that then arises for savers concerns the duration of their gambles and hence their link with the business concerned. If the shares are held for a long time, this points to a trusting, stable relationship – shareholders are then partners rather than speculators.

The shorter the period shares are held for, the more the shareholders become speculators, destabilising rather than stabilising the business's value. Greater volatility means greater risk and hence reduced future share performance.

When shares are held for a short, speculative period, the business simply becomes something to gamble on. The saver has no expectations of the business, but is merely betting on a change in the mood of the market. If, on the other hand, the saver decides to hold the share in the medium term, his expectation and his gamble are based on the business's actual performance and reflect a degree of trust in its management, products or management team. The ethical discussion also requires the saver, or whoever is acting on his behalf, to take account of others – in this case, the listed business.

Against this background, what are we to make of 'short selling' techniques which involve savers committing themselves to sell, on a pre-arranged date and at a pre-arranged price, a share they do not yet actually hold, but that they hope to purchase in the meantime at a lower price than the contracted one? This is speculation, often accompanied by the use of option-type coverage instruments, that prices will fall – potentially very lucrative, but very dangerous for savers, and it helps to destabilise share prices, and indirectly businesses, by driving share prices downwards.

3.7 Asset and risk management institutions

Relatively few savers manage their financial assets without expert aid. Some turn to retail banks, with their ranges of savings and deposit accounts, to life insurance (mentioned earlier) and to pension funds. The wealthiest use specialised agents known as asset managers. With the exception of the latter, other institutions make promises to savers in return for their liquidity.

These institutions must then manage assets that they hold but that have been temporarily entrusted to them so as to keep their promises when the time comes. They must act with strict respect for every client, and without favouring any individual or group. This equal-treatment requirement may seem self-evident, but it is not. In practice, the institutions' commitments are not identical in terms of amounts, dates or income. Some were formulated in different times, when things that are now unthinkable were quite normal. The institutions were thus tempted – sometimes obliged – to make adjustments or even to arbitrate among clients. This is a very delicate aspect of internal management, and arbitration is difficult. Yet it is vital that such decisions be taken by managing bodies, rather left unaddressed or disguised or concealed on false pretexts.

The ethical requirement that the weakest segments should be protected in such cases needs to be recalled here. This requirement conflicts with practices that tend to favour the best clients, that is those with the best business prospects. For this reason, and to control impulses and maintain due discipline, external supervision may therefore be required.

3.8 The role of savings at macroeconomic level

The ultimate fund holder is the main pillar of all financial activity. Hence the importance of the institutional choices made at macro level. Depending on legislative and political options of the moment, financial savings may or may not be preferred to other ways of building up assets, risks will be divided sometimes in favour of the banker and sometimes in favour of the saver, and the weakest may or may not be protected. All these choices are part of social ethics, for they help to create the main ways of distributing resources, income and risks among groups of players.

Without exhausting the question of social ethics, which will be discussed in the next two chapters, three issues that are directly associated with savings will be mentioned here:

- The encouragement of financial savings may use up resources otherwise available for financing entrepreneurial activity and physically building up assets. The most frequently used instruments are guarantees for deposits and guarantees in terms of interest on a limited number of instruments. In adopting such measures, governments guarantee the financial sector a flow of business, while they take on themselves all or part of the risk of a financial meltdown.
- Another ethical choice involves more or less strict control of the products that are likely to be the subject of government appeals to save. Essentially, the aim here is to protect people with limited financial experience from a given level of financial risk – or, on the contrary, expose them to it – and hence to subject them, or not subject them, to the temptation of reward. The more restrictive and controlled the conditions of appeals to save, the less chance there is that the weakest and least educated will fall victim to abuses or confusing promises by service providers.
- The third dimension involving social ethics concerns society's institutional choices regarding pensions and life insurance. As mentioned earlier, retirement and similar schemes permanently reduce the amount of savings that households have at their disposal, while increasing flows towards finance. Whether these are compulsory or voluntary savings schemes, they reduce people's ability to build up assets and hence weaken intergenerational solidarity in favour of collectivisation of savings within major institutions. The consequences of such choices are binding in the very long term. They are reflected in a growing role for the state, which is the direct or indirect guarantor of promises,

and in a stronger (including politically stronger) financial sector, and they weaken family businesses, particularly in their ability (and sometimes will) to grow. Whereas during the Thirty Euphoric Years the pendulum of political solutions clearly swung towards socialisation of savings, the crisis has helped reveal the unexpected consequences of such choices. In the light of what we have seen now that the euphoria has evaporated, a fundamental rethink is therefore urgently needed.[7]

This chapter has reviewed a number of ethical considerations and dilemmas that face savers who use finance to invest or increase their assets. As mentioned on several occasions, savers are necessary, but not sufficient, for finance to take place. The *essential* condition is that those who are ready to purchase promises can come into contact with those who are able to make them. The ethical issues and dilemmas that face the latter will be the subject of the next chapter.

Notes

1 Hans Jonas, *The Imperative of Responsibility: In Search of an Ethics for the Technological Age*, University of Chicago Press, Chicago, 1984 (first published in German in 1979).
2 Dembinski, Paul H., Bonvin, Jean-Michel, Dommen, Edouard, Monnet, François-Marie, 'Ethics Foundations of Responsible Investment', *Journal of Business Ethics*, vol. 48: 203–213, 2003.
3 Paul H. Dembinski (ed.), *Pratiques financières – regards chrétiens*, Desclée de Brouwer, Paris, 2009, particularly the section by Jean-Claude Lavigne; see also John Thomas Noonan, *The Scholastic Analysis of Usury*, Harvard University Press, Cambridge, MA, 1957.
4 For some decades – and the trend has increased since 2007 – major international companies have been accumulating comfortable levels of funds that are similar to savings. Many of them actively manage this liquidity, without any direct link to their core activities, so that the finance function makes a significant – and often very significant – contribution to their overall performance. Such excess liquidity indicates that these companies do not have any credible investment projects in their field and prefer to 'wait and see', perhaps hoping they will be able to acquire something. In any case, their 'refusal' to invest in the real economy and instead use finance to invest funds they cannot otherwise use reminds us of actors' moral duty to use all their resources, without exception, for the creation of wealth.
5 In the last chapter of his *General Theory of Employment, Interest and Money*, Keynes wrote that the overabundance of capital would mean the end of *rentiers* and so put an end to the oppression exerted by holders of (financial) capital.
6 Gabriele Taylor's *Deadly Vices*, Clarendon Press, Oxford, 2006, shows that greed of any kind is the mother of all vices, infecting not only individuals but society as a whole.
7 It is only since the crisis that politicians have become aware of the financial fragility of the SME fabric. This is because savings flows that would otherwise have gone to SMEs were diverted into markets by financial euphoria.

4 The ethical dilemmas facing fund users

Public or private debtors and investors

The other essential component of finance is users of other people's funds. Financial contracts are based on the promises and commitments they make and the prospects they offer. Their gaze is resolutely fixed on what they see as a prosperous future, which in turn depends on reducing present constraints. They do so by signing contracts with fund holders that commit them to future payments. Finance thus allows intertemporal transfers of income and risk, and an escape from the present by acting as if the future were already here. However, the debtor can only 'free up the present' by placing a burden on his future. Thus, far from eliminating constraint, finance only seems to reduce it, and only temporarily. Furthermore, constraints that have been shifted into the future are increased by the interplay of interest.

Debt and, more broadly, search for funding are key parts of our financialised societies. These activities involve households, businesses and public bodies, as do the associated ethical dilemmas. Just as with fund holders, the dilemmas arise simultaneously at various levels: individuals, institutions and societal choices.

4.1 The roots of promises and households' commitments

Aspirations towards a better life are commonplace. They are deeply rooted in contemporary man, who sees the future as a promise of opportunities. Today, globalisation embodies the age-old idea of progress and promises of greater prosperity. This essentially optimistic attitude is characteristic of Western culture which, despite its extensive secularisation, is still permeated by the Christian promise and its corollary: everyone's duty to take an active part in building a better world.

Three kinds of situation and reasons may tempt actors to gain access to other people's funds. These situations need to be clearly distinguished at the outset:

- The first situation is emergency or distress. With his back to the wall, the actor desperately seeks a way out. The only resource available to him in the emergency is his future, which he is forced to put at risk by incurring debt. If the situation really is an emergency, the borrower simply cannot afford to ask himself ethical questions. Yet real emergencies are relatively rare compared with the pseudo-emergencies that consumer society creates by arousing desires so pressing that they are eventually mistaken, often by the weakest, for real emergencies. This is where the loan sharks scent their prey. In cases of emergency and distress, it is thus the lender rather than the borrower who faces an ethical dilemma. The temptation to use human distress or disorientation for easy gain has always attracted usurers, disguised as kind rescuers, and the wrath of moralists.[1]

- The second situation is a convenience/consumer loan. The borrower's dilemma is how to realistically assess the nature of the need/desire that is to be satisfied in the short term compared with the financial burden he commits himself to bearing in the future. He may easily be misled by his view of the future. If his assessment of future income is unduly optimistic, his decision to yield to the temptation of instant convenience is a gamble rather than a promise. Such a gamble may prove irresponsible in two ways. Not only does it put future income at unreasonable risk, thus exposing the borrower to the risk of destitution, but it also exposes the lender – who is often complacent when making the loan – to the risk of losing his money.

- The third situation is funding designed to create added value. The idea here is that the funds invested will generate future resources. For instance, they may help to improve the quality of family life by purchasing a dwelling on credit; they may allow the start of economic activity, or even an actual business, that will hopefully generate a flow of income or allow investment to expand or replace part of an existing business. We will focus here on the family dwelling; the financing of businesses will be discussed in the next section. Borrowing to give one's family a roof over their heads is a structuring decision – as defined in the previous chapter – for it provides a material framework for the development of the next generation and the accompanying sense of security. Since this is a long-term commitment (often for more than twenty years), it is a decision with major implications for families' budgets and equilibrium. The ethical dilemma is therefore particularly great here, especially for the families that have to bear the resulting financial burdens. The risks and consequences of having to sell their home or move house must be considered soberly if future distress is to be avoided. In situations where emotions can easily gain the upper hand, realistic commitment must be clearly distinguished from gambling on future changes in prices or wages.

Loans that create value, especially mortgages, reflect impatience and a wish to speed things up. Although it may seem prudent to save for twenty years in order to avoid taking out a loan when buying a home, this makes no sense at all in the family context, for by the time the money has been saved the children will have moved out. The ethical question raised by such a loan is how to distinguish between gambling and commitment. The former involves speculation on possible futures; the latter a will to find a way of building up a future in keeping with an accomplished life.

There is thus a fundamental difference between taking out a loan to buy a home and hoping that house prices will rise and the dwelling can be resold, and buying the same home on the basis of realistically calculated future income. The latter involves a well-considered promise of reimbursement; the former is a speculative gamble that is often concealed by emotions. A prudent attitude – if adopted by both parties to the contract – should allow an ethical and economically correct diagnosis to be made, and prevent both individual and macroeconomic disaster. The recent example of the American subprime mortgages in 2007 and 2008 reminds us just how costly a lack of ethics and prudence can prove.

In this specific case, the ethical problem was due to a twofold misunderstanding that was more or less intentionally organised by the intermediaries. Neither the debtors nor the final purchasers of the collateralised debt obligations (CDOs) were fully aware that they were gambling on changes in house prices rather than making commitments. The intermediaries made loans to people who were ill-prepared to understand the risks inherent in the gambles they were making; nor did they alert the purchasers of the debts to the ultimate debtors' precarious situations. As a result, the debtors lost their homes, with collateral damage to their families, and the creditors lost part of their money.

4.2 Risk and business financing

As long ago as the eighteenth century, the specific role of entrepreneurs was clearly understood by Richard Cantillon. The entrepreneur, he said, is someone who takes risks on fixed costs. He wrote this at a time in which the legal construct of the 'legal person' was the exception and not – as it is today – the rule.[2] Today, the entrepreneur's financial risk is confined to its invested capital, that is the own capital of the business which corresponds to shares. There are two different kinds of shareholder: entrepreneurs with shares in their own businesses, and outside shareholders who simply provide funding, without any knowledge or particular competence regarding the business's field of activity. The ethical dilemma for the initiator of the entrepreneurial project involves knowing which sources of financing he can reasonably seek without exposing them to excessive risk. This problem arises in the case of family businesses, when savings of family members are used to finance a seemingly brilliant but in practice often badly flawed project. The entrepreneur is then torn between the ease of access to such funding – in which personal trust and the corresponding promise play a key role – and the funder's understanding of the project. The entrepreneur faces the same kind of dilemma when a bank insists on the family home being mortgaged as collateral for a business loan. There are no easy answers here; they must be found by exploring all the alternatives, including changing the way in which the business is funded. This may provide an opportunity to think about fair distribution of risk and responsibility within a wider family community.

4.3 Business financing: the leverage dilemma

Business financing (on the liability side of the balance sheet) can be divided into equity that is ultimately made available by shareholders – including through undistributed profits – and external capital, which essentially means creditors' loans. Leverage measures the ratio of a business's debts to its equity: the higher the share of debts, the greater the leverage.

Each in their own way, shareholders and creditors have placed their trust in the business. The former have shown long-term trust in the economic prospects of a project, the product or service, or the business's management team. The funds they make available to the business are permanently at its disposal, regardless of how things turn out. In return, shareholders become co-owners with a say in what happens and, if things turn out well, entitlement to profits, including additional profits due to the increase in the value of the business, which they can realise by selling their shares to others.

As for creditors, they have shown time-limited trust in the soundness of the business and its ability to honour its contractual commitments to pay back its debts and pay its interest. They are not involved in running the business, and do not intend to replace shareholders when it comes to taking business risks.

Until recently, the rule of sound financial management required businesses to have enough equity to cover the most specific assets of its activity, that is those that have no intrinsic value and would be lost if the business were to fail. This approach also set an appropriate level of leverage and indebtedness for each enterprise. Businesses with insufficient equity to cover assets at risk were in turn considered at risk, and so creditors demanded higher rates of return. Since the late 1970s, however, practice has changed in response to the Modigliani–Miller theorem, which states that leverage has no direct impact on the valuation of the business.[3] Despite this conclusion to which stick still today finance theory, leverage has been used – not to say manipulated – in order to increase managers' and shareholders' remuneration.

Leverage is today seen by the business world, above all as a way to increase return on a business's equity. The idea is a simple one: if the average return on a business's total assets (regardless of where its funding comes from) exceeds the rate of interest on its debts, shareholders should – all other things being equal – incur more debt. This is because the difference between the average return on capital and the interest paid on each additional unit of debt directly increases shareholder profits. Leverage can thus been seen as a way to pump up return on equity or, in other words, to improve the present for shareholders and managers; meanwhile, however, the business's future is at risk. Conversely, if the return on equity is lower than rates of interest on debts, the interest paid to creditors eats into profits. In that case, shareholders are 'subsidising' creditors.

This being the case, in unperfect makets and despite the Modigliani–Miller theorem, leverage also affects – again, all other things being equal – the level of risk that the business poses to creditors. The lower the share of equity, the more vulnerable the business is to cyclical changes, for any losses must be absorbed by equity. The lower this is, the greater the risk that the business will fail, with a direct impact on creditors. The level of leverage therefore determines the distribution of risks between shareholders and creditors. Determining the optimum level of indebtedness therefore confronts businesses' management teams with an ethical dilemma, for they are forced to weigh up shareholders' and creditors' interests.

The ethical dilemma facing managers is that they may be induced to increase indebtedness beyond what is reasonable and thus expose the creditor to risks that the latter, being external to the business, cannot fully assess. Managers may be all the more tempted to expose the creditor to more risk without his knowledge because this benefits shareholders, on whom managers – and their remuneration, which is often linked to the return on equity – directly depend.

4.4 The discount rate dilemma

When choosing which investment projects to finance, business managers may therefore face an ethical dilemma: which discount rate they use to evaluate projects. In theory, this is based on the weighted average of levels of remuneration expected by shareholders and creditors respectively.[4] In practice, the more generous the business wishes to be towards its sources of funding, the higher the discount rate will be. However, given the mechanics of discount rate, higher (positive) it is, greater priority will then automatically go to projects with short-term rewards, at the expense of medium- and long-term projects. The higher the discount rate chosen, the lower the current value of more remote payments. In other words, the higher the rate, the shorter the economically pertinent time horizon.

The dilemma is that this type of calculation technique stands on an ethical choice that benefits for shareholders at the expense of the business's medium- and long-term survival. Such choices regarding investment projects are often influenced by the fact that managers' remunerations are linked to stock-exchange prices: managers may then be tempted to endanger other stakeholders in the business, particularly its employees, in the long term. Here again, whoever is responsible for using funds must find the courage to get away from purely technical calculations and see the dilemma in ethical terms, in the light of his own room for manoeuvre.

4.5 Public fund users

Like households and businesses, public bodies may also have good reasons to use other people's funds, whether these be bank loans or the bond market. These reasons are in every way similar to those facing households: emergencies (war, disasters, epidemics, etc.), or loans that improve people's standards of living while enabling politicians to show voters the tangible impact of their governance. Finally, loans may be needed to fund investments likely to have a long-term impact on growth, and so increase future tax revenues.

The ethical dilemmas facing those in charge of public finances essentially involve the latter two kinds of reasons to incur debt. Three of these dilemmas may be mentioned here.

The first concerns the relationship between electoral issues and the state of public finances. Some public expenditures and investments have a twofold impact: the costs of implementing a project that gives politicians greater prominence, and the operating costs that place a lasting burden on public funds. The dilemma facing politicians is how to weigh up what is good for them and their political party in electoral terms, and what is useful and bearable for the public budget in the long term. Some politicians' notions of their own 'accomplished lives' clash with the need to serve others and establish just institutions. Just like business managers, local or national politicians are the only people with all the necessary information to resolve these dilemmas. Some of the resulting decisions have a long-term impact on public finances.

The second dilemma concerns the financial techniques used to raise the funds, as well as the correct assessment of risks and the way in which the corresponding instruments are recorded in accounts. The use of certain kinds of loans, for instance in foreign currencies, may considerably reduce the apparent debt-service burden, but at the same time exposes the community to exchange-rate fluctuations it cannot control. This is the same as the earlier distinction between gambles and promises: gambling on the exchange rate of the foreign currency, and a realistic promise of reimbursement at an agreed rate. Similarly, preferring renewable leasing at a variable rate to loan or investment of public funds may seem more profitable in the short term, but is riskier in the medium term. Once again, there is a parallel between managers who focus on the way their bonuses are calculated and politicians who focus on forthcoming elections. This highlights the ethical dimension of the dilemma. Arbitration between the short and long term is anything but a technical matter.

The third dilemma for politicians and those responsible for public finance concerns the funding of very large investment projects that extend over the long term. By their very nature, financial projections on such projects are inevitably subject to inaccuracies that make it very difficult to reach decisions on them. These natural difficulties are sometimes compounded by economic and political interests that seek to underestimate the short-term costs in order to get the go-ahead for the project. Once the project is launched, the costs are revised upwards; but by then it is too late and too politically risky to stop it, and the community has no choice but to helplessly accept cost overruns. Such situations carry ethical dilemmas. Decision-makers must learn to to avoid being captured by a technical framework that the businesses directly concerned may want to lock them into, and to strike a proper balance between their own egos and the good of the community they are responsible for.

4.6 The ethical aspects of information asymmetry

Using other people's funds creates information asymmetry between the final owner and the user of the funds. This applies to all kinds of credit and to shareholders who are not directly involved in managing the businesses they are funding. In theory, such asymmetry creates opportunities to abuse the funder's good faith – something supposedly controlled by three kinds of mesoeconomic mechanisms:

- The first and most important of these is trust. In the field of finance, it sometimes involves the person or the company's name as the 'signature' of the fund user, sometimes his project and sometimes the legal context in which the contract is drawn up. All these dimensions of trust coexist, although each takes place in a register of its own: the interpersonal register, the economic register, the legal register and, finally, the institutional register. The relative importance of these registers of trust varies from case to case and from period to period.

- The second is guarantees or collateral. The creditor thus has a tangible element that limits his losses if the project fails or the debtor disappears or goes bankrupt. The less trust there is, the greater the importance of guarantees when signing the contract. However, unlike trust, which benefits both parties to the contract, collateral increases the debtor's risk while reducing – or even eliminating – the creditor's. Guarantees and collateral carry an ethical dimension that should not be underestimated, especially when making loans to the poorest members of society.

- The third is the provision of accurate, reliable information on the debtor's economic and financial state. Two different cases may be distinguished here: loans to individuals or small businesses, and loans to well-established businesses and public bodies. The latter case will be discussed in the next section. Banks now require their debtors – whether individuals or businesses – to provide regular details of their finances, failing which their accounts will be closed. Without knowing everything, creditors thus have ways of detecting the debtor's problems before they become apparent. Such information should induce banks to help debtors overcome their difficulties. In practice, however, creditors often take the easy way out and cancel the contract, or demand the guarantee without caring what happens to the debtor. This makes debtors reluctant to be honest with their creditors. The result may be a spiral of distrust, with damaging long-term effects. The associated ethical dilemmas are obvious, but go beyond the scope of this book.

4.7 Accounting conventions and the importance of judgement

Accounting standards aim to reduce information asymmetry between internal operators and the outside world, particularly financial partners. The fact that there are differing standards at global level – for both businesses and public bodies – reveals the limitations of the exercise, for no standard, however precise, can access reality directly, without human intermediation. Moreover, human action may shape reality so as to produce one accounting picture rather than another. Accounting is thus a transcription technique which, like all techniques, is merely an instrument at the service of what are sometimes multiple aims. The ethical dilemma is thus very much part of the accounting professions, auditing and actuarial services.

This is illustrated by three situations:

- The scope of consolidation. Complex businesses, as well as public bodies, may be tempted to keep less glamorous aspects of their activities out of the spotlight. To do so, they sometimes set up entities that are legally outside the scope of consolidation but, in operational terms, are entirely dependent on the main actor. The clash between operational reality and the way it is recorded in legal and accounting terms is an ethical issue, which sometimes confronts managers with profound dilemmas as to which scope of consolidation is ethically relevant. Merely complying with the law is not necessarily enough to provide accurate, reliable information on the state of the business or public body concerned. There are two examples of this. The first, from the financial sector, concerns the special purpose vehicles (SPVs) that are used for structured products; the second, from the public sector, concerns the way in which parabudgetary entities are, or are not, included in public accounts.
- The methods used to value certain assets. The financial crisis has shown the extent to which valuations of certain illiquid assets exceeded their market value. Fanciful overvaluations cost the taxpayer staggering amounts of money. They were made possible by a unique combination of circumstances, each of which had an ethical dimension: the carelessness of rating agencies, the use of deliberately over-optimistic models, operators' herd behaviour, regulators' lack of vigilance, or the headlong pursuit of success at all costs. The ethical dilemmas associated with the choice of methods used to determine 'fair value' are at the heart of all economic and financial activity.
- Income management. This is of particular concern to listed businesses that wish to maintain, year after year, a degree of continuity in their performance in order to reassure others about the continuing stable expansion of their business, and to avoid fluctuating taxation. Such businesses may be tempted to seek (and find) ways of transferring some of their income from 'fat' years to later years that seem likely to be more 'lean'. Keeping entirely within the law, the business will send its invoices earlier or later, put funds aside or not, and find new ways to pay off, or not pay off, debts. Each of these choices is in line with the business's interests – and those of its management – but is potentially damaging to the quality of information available to third parties, especially its financial partners.

The central factor in each of the above examples is the judgement of those who record reality in an accounting convention. It implies both a deep understanding of the situation and a high level of ethical responsibility based on a limited number of general professional principles. Yet the current trend in the accounting professions is in the opposite direction – it involves seeking more and more detailed rules and standards and so reducing professionals' scope to use their informed judgement. In this way, professionals can protect themselves against the risk of being sued for damages, and at the same time abdicate their ethical responsibility, relying instead on knee-jerk techniques. This development may increase rather than reduce information asymmetry between the fund users and their sources, and may potentially increase the risk to which the latter are exposed.

4.8 The usury rate

The question of the maximum permitted rate of interest on loans – the usury rate – has been constantly discussed since antiquity. This very sensitive issue distinguishes normal financial activity from abuse and extortion. Legislation on the subject – often referred to as interest rate restrictions – reflects a concern to protect the weakest without obstructing free competition. In France, for instance, since 2003 there is no longer an official usury rate; it has been replaced by 'usury threshold' for each type of financial operation, calculated according to formula based on the relevant market rates.[5] The Bank of France is required to update the results of this calculation every quarter in order to determine the usury rate.

In France, the idea of abandoning a ceiling rate in favour of a formula applicable to each category of transaction was adopted particularly in response to pressure from microfinance institutions, which argued that an absolute rate was pointless in operations involving those excluded from normal finance, and that it would be wiser to mark the boundary of usury by weighing up the various interests in microbusinesses' operating accounts. Microfinance involves lending very small amounts over relatively short periods. Despite their high unit costs, reflecting the high costs of microfinance together with monitoring and assistance, such loans do not endanger the operation of the business – on the contrary, they make it possible.

The ethical debate on abuses in lending activities must thus take account not only of the legal provisions, but also of fair distribution of risks and burdens between the protagonists. In this context, references to 'market rates' may be problematic, for they leave little scope for solutions adapted to individual cases. Far from resolving the issue, 'market rates' make the ethical debate more difficult.

4.9 Ways out when things go wrong: the macro level

Most funding takes place according to agreed contracts without any major problems. However, some promises and commitments are not kept, and some gambles fail. Although few in number, they are potentially a source of conflict and hence are in the public domain. The way in which the established institutional order organises responsibilities and distributes losses among actors involves the field of social ethics and the associated dilemmas.

The risk taken by the debtor involves an obligation to honour the contractual provisions in all circumstances, whether this concerns the specific project or the overall context. In some cases, it may therefore involve removing resources from debtor's assets – indeed, this is the meaning of the guarantee. Paying back the debt may therefore expose the debtor – the household, business or public body – to damages that are incommensurate with the sum lent, such as confiscation of the production tool, starvation or quite simply extinction (for instance if a business goes bankrupt). In such situations, two different logics are in open conflict: the contractual logic of numbers on which the creditor's claims are based, and the logic of life – and survival – that guides the debtor.

The legislator's ethical dilemma involves establishing priority between these two logics in the event of an insurmountable conflict, that is when the parties' goodwill, and contractual ways of restructuring the debt, are exhausted. The law allows creditors certain means of pressure to get their money back from debtors, but contemporary legal arrangements also restrict creditors' scope to exert pressure, at which point the law provides protection for debtors (legal persons) who are in difficulty. Although this principle is widely accepted, there is little unity of doctrine on the subject even between the countries of the European Union, given their very different national practices and traditions. The range of possibilities goes from voluntary declaration of personal bankruptcy (in Britain) to protection against overindebtedness (in France). At this stage, in both cases, creditors are forced to abandon their claims in order to guarantee everyone's inalienable right to a future. Society thus implicitly imposes the principle that both parties share responsibility for a credit contract.

In the case of legal persons, recent revisions in European legislation have tended to give priority to survival of economic substance and jobs over the ruthless dismantling of businesses in creditors' interests. The range of theoretical possibilities include the famous Chapter 11 of the US Bankruptcy Code, which shields struggling businesses from their creditors for a certain period of time.

As for infra-state public bodies, some national legislation provides for thresholds that require overindebted bodies to be placed under supervision and, in some cases, their debts to be reduced.

There are no such provisions in international law. As things stand, it includes no general requirement to protect those owed money by sovereign debtors, other than possible arbitration clauses. Echoing the civil-society 'Jubilee 2000' campaign to cancel developing countries' debts, the International Monetary Fund (IMF) has drawn up a list of criteria: the ratio of debt servicing to export receipts, and the share of debt in GNP. The result is a procedure that aims to relieve the debt owed, mostly to Western governments, by heavily indebted poor countries. Today, 35 countries have made use of this scheme to relieve a total of 75 billion dollars' worth of debt while 41 billion dollars of relief has been granted by multilateral organisations.[6]

The repeated sovereign-debt crisis in the eurozone countries has revealed the absence of a mechanism for reducing indebtedness. This demonstrates that absolute respect for contracts was one of the fundamental ethical choices made by the architects of the European structure. As the European debt crisis has made clear, unless this choice is revised, it will may lead to exclusion of the weakest and, effectively, the end of the solidarity pact.

4.10 The Jubilee project: keeping financial due dates under control

The Jubilee idea belongs to a view of time that is diametrically opposed to the one now governing the fate of today's economy. Jubilee time is exogenous to the economy, and the economy wholly depends on it, without any possible exceptions. For instance, the imperative relief of debts and the restitution of confiscated assets, announced 'every fiftieth year', place a limit on contracts that is in no way endogenous and goes beyond all economic considerations.

By fixing a time horizon that no debt contract can override, the Jubilee idea requires creditors, and debtors, to reason and calculate within a finite timeframe – indeed, verses of the chapter 25 of Leviticus say this in so many words. If the creditor has not recovered what he is owed by the time of the Jubilee, he has no choice but say goodbye to it. As for the debtor, the goods he has lost to the creditor are returned when the Jubilee comes. The Jubilee thus belongs to a very different approach from the 'classic' solution that is adopted in the event of failure to repay. Unlike the contemporary practice that tends to saddle the debtor with a major share of responsibility for the failure, the Jubilee explicitly punishes the imprudent creditor. The Jubilee idea refutes the idea of hesitating between the logic of figures and contracts and the logic of life and survival; instead, it resolutely opts in favour of the survival of the community and rejects exclusion because of debts.

Notes

1 See Archbishop of Canterbury Justin Welby's recent condemnation of Britain's 'payday sharks', who are now making a killing by issuing loans at very high rates of interest.
2 Richard Cantillon, *Essai sur la nature du commerce en général* (1755), recently translated into English as *An Essay on Economic Theory* (Ludwig von Mises Institute, Auburn, AL, 2010).
3 'The Cost of Capital, Corporation Finance and the Theory of Investment', in *American Economic Review*, June 1958.
4 Weighted Average Cost of Capital (WACC).
5 According to Article L. 313-3 of the French Consumer Code, 'any contractual loan granted at an annual percentage rate which, at the time of its granting, is more than one third higher than the average percentage rate applied by the credit institutions during the previous quarter for loans of the same type presenting a similar risk factor . . . constitutes a usurious loan.'

   For an assessment of usury legislation in the European Union, see *Study on Interest Rate Restrictions in the EU*, by Udo Reifner, Sebastien Clerc-Renaud, RA Michael Knobloch, Hamburg, 2009, Institut für Finanzdienstleistungen e.V. (iff) (http://ec.europa.eu/internal_market/finservices-retail/docs/credit/irr_report_en.pdf)
6 https://www.imf.org/external/np/pp/eng/2014/121214.pdf.

5 Ethical dilemmas in financial intermediation

The complex apparatus of contemporary financial intermediation draws its *raison d'être* and economic survival from the balancing function that it performs between the owners of temporarily idle funds and potential users and initiators of projects. The specific ethical dilemmas facing each of these two groups have been discussed in the previous chapters. It is now time to look at the specific situations of the actors in the threefold intermediation performed by finance. The first intermediation may be termed 'spatial', for it takes place between actors with complementary aims; the second is 'temporal', for it concerns the adjustment between due dates and the various actors' expectations; and the third concerns risk profiles. This threefold intermediation enables the financial sector to perform its twofold social mission, as an allocator of both capital and risks.

Unlike in the previous chapters, this discussion of ethical dilemmas will first focus on the macro level, presenting the ethical premises and consequences of the two main traditions of financial organisation. Only then will it look at the major ethical dilemmas that arise in finance proper.

5.1 Banks or markets: an alternative made irrelevant by globalisation

Despite nearly half a century of financial globalisation, the institutions and operating procedures in national financial systems still bear marks of the two main historical traditions that are customarily known as the 'credit-based economy' and the 'financial-market economy'.[1] The distinction focuses on the way in which finance is rooted in the whole of economic activity. The organisation of finance in the credit-based economy focuses on the survival of credit and deposit relations based on banks, whereas in the financial-market economy the system is based on market transactions.

In a credit-based economy, the bank is the intermediating institution *par excellence*. It is the gateway through which households and businesses gain access to retail financial services. Banks collect deposits and grant credit without providers of funds and initiators of projects having to meet. At the upper levels of the system, banks trade among each other, which enables them to perform the threefold balancing function between their clients' initially disparate maturities, amounts and risks. In return for services rendered, banks are remunerated by the differential between debtor and creditor interest and by commissions. Although the 'credit-based economy' version of the financial system has never existed in its pure form, the organisation of finance in continental or (to use the term coined by Michel Albert) 'Rhine' economies has emerged from this tradition – particularly in Germany, Spain, France, Italy, Switzerland and, in some respects, Japan.

In a financial-market economy, the market is the place where contracts are made between owners and potential users of funds. The financial professions then act as agents and facilitators for encounters between actors with complementary needs, schedules and risk profiles; but they do not assume direct responsibility and so – unlike classic banks in the credit-based economy – do not become parties to the contract. This being the case, contracts, stocks and securities serve as raw materials for trade, in which the threefold balancing function is performed by seeking direct complementarities. Securities thus frequently change hands, contract law ensuring that all the seller's rights and commitments are transferred to the purchaser without consequences for, or interference by, the financed entity.

In the 'market', the initiator of the project will not be permanently linked to a single financier, but will face an anonymous mass of nomadic financiers who are all potentially ready to enter or leave the relevant relationship, depending on shifting prospects, prices and risk levels. Conversely, the owner of funds can keep adjusting his positions. The organisation of finance around the market thus gives rise to a huge volume of transactions in existing assets. Most transactions (over 95 per cent) on OECD stock markets involve the transfer of already circulating securities, and fund-raising for new projects is only a marginal proportion of the total. The typical organisation financial-market economy has never existed in the pure state; nor indeed has that of the credit-based economy. However, the organisation of finance based on the market is unquestionably part of the 'Anglo-Saxon' tradition.

Each of the two traditions of financial organisation is based on different social choices, in at least three key respects:

- The locus of responsible financial action: the Anglo-Saxon tradition emphasises that users of other people's funds and their owners bear ultimate responsibility for their actions. Whereas, in the Rhine tradition, banks have traditionally had a paternalistic responsibility to guide and advise.

- A different typology of financial actors: the Rhine tradition tends to distinguish between three strata, namely the general public with little financial expertise, sophisticated seekers of financial services who are able to cope, and peer professionals employed by financial institutions. In the Anglo-Saxon tradition, the first two strata tend to merge, leaving only professionals who provide financial services and clients who seek them.

- A different central stabiliser of the system: the truth and effectiveness of financial prices (in both the ethical and the technical sense) are the key elements in financial markets – otherwise the dice are loaded, decisions are flawed, and actors can no longer assume their responsibilities. The ethical integrity of the market is therefore essential. Things are different in the Rhine tradition, in which the soundness of banks is crucial. The professionalism of intermediation is reflected in the soundness of their balance sheets. Apart from the differences, what the two traditions have in common is the fact that the health of the system depends on financial professionals' integrity – and on regulators' shrewdness.

Financial globalisation is causing the two traditions to merge. The result is a two-level system based on two main factors:

- the emergence of global financial conglomerates, known for convenience as 'universal' banks, that is banks that perform all the financial functions. We are talking here about a few dozen mega-actors. Indeed, in 2011 the Financial Stability Board identified them by name as 'global systemically important financial institutions';

- the interconnection of financial markets around the globe through technology, and the ubiquitous presence of these mega-actors.

There are thus two levels of activity in the emerging organisation of world finance: the local level and the global level. Part of the threefold intermediation process takes place on the spot, at the local – national – level. What cannot be done there is then 'repackaged' by the mega-actors and moved to the upper level of the system: global markets. This financial wholesale market is where global players' bank balance sheets are adjusted, states and major concerns raise funds and the relevant securities are traded. At the local level, the institutions that have emerged from indigenous traditions and practices act as retailers: they perform some of their intermediation on the spot, but they add up the remaining savings balances and transfer them to global markets, where they seek refinancing by offering risk profiles and investments with local connotations – which are of interest to global players in search of uncorrelated assets.

The current merger of the two traditions as a result of financial globalisation is taking place at the expense of the organisational logic of the credit-based economy, which is losing its power. Thus, in all the countries with this tradition, the local role of financial markets and dependence on global markets were constantly increasing during the Thirty Euphoric Years.

The decline of the Rhine tradition in finance can also be seen on an intellectual level: modern financial theory largely ignores banks and focuses instead on financial markets. It is only since the crisis that sound bank balance sheets have regained their importance and attract much attention of monetary authorities, scholars and regulators alike.

The merger has also affected the ethical perspectives genuine to each of the two traditions, hence the current multiplicity of approaches on the subject. A complete synthesis between the two traditions of addressing ethics in finance has yet to come. This awkward situation should not be forgotten in the following discussion. It concerns the ethical dilemmas inherent in contemporary financial intermediation, which arise – albeit in different ways – in both traditions.

5.2 Advise, prescribe or sell?

In his relationship with the final client, the financial professional acts as a provider of services or a seller of financial products. In branches of European banks the 'advisor' has increasingly replaced the seller. This shift in terminology points to an ambiguity and an ethical dilemma that need to be explored. What is the function of the 'advisor'? Should he advise, prescribe or sell?

In societies in which two thirds of national income come from service activities and are knowledge-generated, advisors, experts and agents are ubiquitous. In many areas we need additional knowledge in order to solve a problem or reach a decision. This is not so much lack of information – the asymmetry of information discussed in the previous chapter – as inability to use the available information correctly. We are thus dealing with asymmetry of understanding rather than lack of information.

In resorting to experts – whether they be bankers, lawyers, garage mechanics, accountants or doctors – clients are looking for expertise that will help them decide how to proceed. Yet advisers often slip into the role of prescribers – particularly prescribers of their own services. They are advisors, prescribers and – ultimately – sellers, which potentially puts them in a situation of 'conflicting interests'. This term describes the clash between two potentially diverging motivations that may confront the expert: his client's best interests, and concern for his own turnover and the related objectives set by his superiors. There is nothing new about such situations – what is new is their extension to every facet of life, owing to their extreme sophistication. Furthermore, traditional professional bodies have drawn up rules of ethics that lay down their professional duties. In some cases, candidates for the profession are even examined to identify those whose characters enable them to overcome conflicts and put their professional integrity and their clients' best interests first. A classic example is the Hippocratic Oath sworn by doctors.

There is no ethical dilemma of conflicting interests if the client can be assumed to have all the resources he needs to understand where his interest lies, to make informed judgements and to reach decisions freely. Such a client is assumed to know that the service window in a bank is there to sell services, and that the advice he will be given is bound to be slanted. If the client then buys the service, it is because he believes that is where his interest lies. In that case, the advisor-prescriber-seller has no conflict of interests.[2]

The fundamental question here is whether the hypothesis of the perfectly lucid, informed client can be confirmed. In other words, we need to know whether financial intermediation implies a fiduciary duty for the professional, or is quite simply a commercial activity.

- In the former case, there is a fiduciary duty and the professional is morally obliged to put the client's best interests first, even if the client is unable to put them into words. In doing so, the professional must eliminate any asymmetry of understanding.
- In the latter case, the *caveat emptor* ('let the buyer beware') principle applies. The professional does not then need to worry about the client's ability to understand, but must simply ensure that the client is correctly informed about what he is buying. The professional need only ensure that asymmetry of information is not excessive.

The question of fiduciary duty arises case by case, but requires an overall answer. How is the client seen in legal terms? This will determine which client approach and business model are adopted by the bank and any other financial institution. It will also affect how aggressively sales goals are set and rewarded. Clearly, having to acknowledge a fiduciary duty places a greater constraint on the financial professions; so of course they prefer the purely contractual view based on the hypothesis of equally competent parties. Indeed, it is in this direction that practice – if not legislation – appears to be developing.[3]

Drawing the client's profile in general terms in no way reduces the specific ethical dilemma facing an account manager whose superiors are pushing him to sell products he considers unsuitable or even damaging for a client that trusts him. The account manager knows his client personally, and knows his ability, or inability, to grasp the subtleties of the product being sold; and he would no doubt have preferred the less ambiguous role of the seller rather than the prescriber who enjoys his client's trust – especially when choosing long-term investments for the client's lifetime savings. The employer could help his employees solve such dilemmas honourably. Instead, in the interests of protecting turnover, superiors often choose not to, and leave their employees to handle their dilemmas unaided.

The question of conflicts of interest and the accompanying ethical dilemmas becomes more acute in the case of cross-selling, in which the business model – with its ad hoc goals and remuneration systems – always tries to make clients purchase products and services they were not a priori intending to buy.

In modern finance, the question of conflicting interests has at least three ethical repercussions:

- The ethical status of the financial professions: the question is whether these professions – and, if so, which ones – should enjoy a particular professional status. This would create a duty of loyalty towards the client, and a social task. If this were widely adopted,[4] financial institutions would be required to respect their employees' autonomy of judgement whenever an ethical dilemma arises.
- Remuneration structure: remuneration and the prospect of professional advancement tend to make employees avoid paying too much attention to ethical dilemmas that arise in the course of their work. Transparency about intermediaries' sources of remuneration (especially kick-backs and other inducements received from third parties) and incentives are a key item of information for users, who would then be in a better position to identify gaps in the information provided and any bias in favour of certain solutions or products. Transparency on these issues would not eliminate conflicts of interest, but it would reduce their damaging effects.
- Conflicts of interest inherent in organisational structure: if the same entity is responsible for an IPO (initial public offering) of one client while managing other clients' asset portfolios, there is a great temptation to include the new securities in the portfolios. The loyalty and impartiality promised by the asset management contract are then undermined by the lure of the commission. Even if complementarity between the two activities allows what are known in business jargon as 'synergies', there is an institutionalised conflict of interests. A mere employee is unable to control such a situation, for it is built into the business model. The idea of internal 'firewalls' that supposedly keep the various activities, performed within the same enterprises, sealed

off from each other has shown its limitations. This raises the question of whether conflicts of interest inherent in organisational structure are legally acceptable. Hence the current debate on how – within one and the same conglomerate – investment bank activities can be isolated from other activities such as asset management and retail banking.

5.3 Financial innovation: *cui bono?*

Financial innovation, spurred by technological progress and conceptual breakthroughs in financial theory, was one of the key features of the Thirty Euphoric Years – although assessments of it have varied. For instance, the former Chairman of the US Federal Reserve, Paul Volcker, is alleged to have said that the only truly useful financial innovation in the contemporary era was the ATM.[5]

Financial products can roughly be divided into two main categories: standard and non-standard products. The former are governed by regulations (e.g. France's *Livret A* savings scheme) or traded on organised markets (shares), whereas the latter are not governed by specific regulations and are traded over the counter. The same is true of markets and institutions: some are subject to financial supervision, and require a banking licence, whereas others ('shadow banking') are beyond the reach of regulators.

The innovation that indisputably revolutionised modern finance was the spread of derivative products and the emergence, from the 1970s onwards, of organised markets for them. The real innovation was the development in 1973, by three future Nobel prizewinners (Black, Merton and Scholes), of a now standard formula for pricing options. This particular type of contract creates the possibility, but not the obligation, to perform a predetermined transaction at an agreed price and at a time specified in advance. Standardisation opened the door to the spread of trade in options. These instruments in turn allowed finance's 'risk allocation' function to become autonomous. Modern finance is inconceivable without derivatives – a radical innovation that is attractive to both holders of idle cash balances and intermediaries. It enables everyone to protect himself against fluctuations in stock prices, exchange rates and interest rates. The ethical question that faces asset managers is how to use these costly tools in a reasonable way, particularly when dealing with clients who have entrusted the management of funds to them.

Ad hoc derivatives based on a highly sophisticated statistical and formal apparatus were soon able to flourish in the intellectually fertile soil of standard (plain vanilla) derivatives. These products became many intermediaries' stock-in-trade. They were also widely used by institutions whose boards of directors had difficulty in understanding how they worked.

This created an obvious ethical dilemma: to what extent can you authorise the use of an instrument whose effects – and particularly risks – you yourself do not fully understand? The technical pressures may be high, and so may the pressures from decision-makers. Such pressures tend to conceal the real question: *cui bono*? Who really benefits from these products – the sellers or designers of the products, or also their users, even if they do not understand the technique involved? Given such asymmetry of understanding, the professional bears considerable ex-ante responsibility, although he often refuses to acknowledge it.

Another, more recent wave of financial innovation involved 'structured' products. The idea was to put together a 'package' of similar commitments that were otherwise independent of each other. By combining these, financial engineers created assets with exceptional risk/reward parameters that were unparalleled in the ordinary financial world. No one seemed to doubt the value of these instruments – until the crisis revealed the limitations, including ethical ones, of the underlying models. The ethical dilemma of how such products distributed risks, rewards and commissions among end users was concealed by the economic success of the technique and its benefits for the intermediaries involved. The ethical implications of using such products for transferring risk to people who did not understand it and were incapable of bearing it are now only too obvious.

The very term 'financial innovation' suggests it must be a good thing. Yet the main (but unadmitted) purpose of financial innovation is often to generate commissions – which are scarcely visible from outside – for those who provide the services. What made the ethical dilemma easier to ignore was that users were assumed to understand the technique and to have all the information they needed. So the products were sold without any qualms. Some asset managers resisted the temptation of inducements proposed by product developers, preferring to put the final client's interests first. However, such decisions were seldom individual; they were part of the institution's policy, and involved many people.

All this explains why there are now increasing calls for regulation to fill the ethical gaps, and for users to be protected against misuse of financial innovations by a certification system which, just as with medicines, tests the product and assesses its effectiveness before authorising its distribution.

5.4 The quality of prices: insider trading, market rigging and dark pools

In the Anglo-Saxon financial tradition, market integrity is crucial. Compliance with the rules that make sure the market runs smoothly is therefore of the greatest ethical importance. Two kinds of event are likely to derail a market: the spread of off-market transactions, and insider trading. In order for a market to be technically efficient, all transactions involving a given product must take place within the market, and all operators must have the same information about it. Only then will the price have the required economic and ethical quality.

Dark pools threaten the quality of prices. Obviously, if demand remains constant, the price of a kilo of tomatoes will differ depending on whether ten, a hundred or a thousand tonnes of them are on sale. The same applies to financial markets: if some transactions take place off-market, the market price will not be a true reflection of supply and demand, and will therefore be distorted, in both economic and ethical terms. Yet the quality of prices should be a matter of universal concern, for everyone's decisions depend on it. Until the early 1990s, markets were organised like cooperatives; they were collective non-for-profit institutions. In the mid-1990s, however, the demutualisation of stock exchanges began, and they became listed companies. At the same time, they started to refine their price structure favouring their best, and often largest, clients and so on. As a result, people began to steer clear of stock exchanges, not only because of the costs but also because the new technologies allowed them to conduct transactions outside organised markets. This shift towards private clearing and transaction systems – among them 'dark pools' – raised questions about the quality of prices on organised markets, and created a major ethical dilemma for individual operators, the profession and society as a whole.

The fact that it is cheaper for a market player to use a price already determined in an organised market as a basis for conducting private transactions than to use the market and pay commissions is a purely micro-economic argument. The ethical issue at stake is very different. In pursuing their own narrow interests, by by-passing the market operators are depriving it of important information. Without expressly wishing to, they are distorting the market and thus – indirectly – misleading the entire community. The ethical dilemma becomes evident as soon as we look beyond mere agent's costs. We are now witnessing an explosion in the number of untransparent transactions on 'closed platforms' – a development that is undermining the ethical and economic hypothesis of the market promise as an unbiased and thus efficient allocator of resources.

The efficient-market hypothesis recently received a further battering with the discovery of collusion between operators to manipulate the two cornerstones of world finance: LIBOR (the London Interbank Offered Rate) and the foreign-exchange market. In the case of LIBOR the manipulation did not involve actual market transactions, but information about the rates that would probably have been applied if transactions had taken place.

This information, which is published daily, is of crucial importance, for it determines the prices of all the contracts that use LIBOR as their reference. Its impact extends to retail clients, for example through variable-rate mortgages. What made this scam so shocking was its scale: by the time it came to light in 2012, a dozen global banks had been involved in it for several years. The idea behind manipulating LIBOR was to protect or favour positions taken by some of the banks concerned or by individual traders – operators' personal friends – especially at critical moments in the financial crisis. The entire financial world was deliberately misled.

In the foreign exchange scam, the world's largest over-the-counter market appears to have been manipulated by operators working for the world's largest banks. The earliest information dates from 2013, and at the time of writing it is not yet clear whether the culprits were acting on their superiors' instructions or on their own, or friends, account.

Maintaining the equality of information is vital. The authorities in charge of organised markets impose whopping fines on anyone who derives unfair benefits from insider trading. The corollary of equality of prices for all operators is strict equality of information, for only then can the various purchase and sales orders be based on the same situation. If some people know more than others, there is no longer a single frame of reference and market integrity falls apart. The 'quality of prices' issue raised here is the same as in the previous case, and so is the ethical dilemma: by using insider information, operators obtain benefits for themselves, but at the expense of the community and the integrity of the market, which sends a misleading signal.

The recent spread of high-frequency trading (HFT) illustrates the ethical problems raised by the quality of prices.[6] The operators involved have incredibly high-powered computers that can detect a purchase or sales order before other operators become aware of it. The software then makes 'flash orders' that are cancelled a few milliseconds after they are sent; their sole purpose is to make the algorithm on the computer that issued the initial order conclude the transaction at a slightly better price than if the flash orders had not been made. The owner of the HFT software uses it to take advantage of less well-equipped buyers or sellers, who are unable to avoid such hi-tech traps. The ethical dilemma raised by the use of this technically superior equipment is only too obvious. Just as clearly, operators who deliberately use such techniques to 'beat out' anyone unfortunate enough to be on the receiving end will have no qualms about it. At the same time, like insider trading, such practices distort market prices at the margin. All this raises the question of whether government regulation is required in order to protect market integrity.

5.5 Volatility and risk transfer

As has been said on several occasions, modern finance developed around the notion of risk operationalised by Harry Markowitz during the 1950s. According to this approach, the level of risk is measured by 'volatility', that is price variability over a given period of time. Volatility has thus become the key variable in modern finance, determining whether or not to use risk coverage and management instruments such as options and other derivatives. This means that volatility is a source of risk for ultimate funds' owners or users and a market opportunity for sellers of risk coverage strategies.

The end users of financial services – initiators of projects and holders of cash balances – mainly live in the real economy, whose rhythm is seasonal, monthly or, at most, daily. In contrast, financial markets unceasingly reassess – 24 hours a day – the value of promises, commitments and gambles in the light of the constant flow of new information. This combination of a constant flow of information with markets that are permanently on the alert automatically creates price instability – volatility – without the primary users of financial services being concerned. In turn, the volatility that is now in the genes of modern finance sucks in demand for risk management and coverage strategies, leading to the purchase of derivatives. Since the latter life-span is limited by the exercise date, their purchases must be regularly repeated. We are reminded here of the arsonist firefighter: does maintaining volatility provide a way for finance, particularly through its risk management function, to make itself indispensable and, by the way, generate commissions? This question goes beyond the ethical dilemma, for it challenges one of the dogmas of contemporary finance.

As regards risk management, banks also face the temptation of transferring risks from their balance-sheets to their clients. They do this by suggesting to certain segments of their clientele – in return for possibly higher rewards – that they reduce their deposit or savings accounts and instead buy products (shares in various kinds of investment funds) that are often produced by the bank itself. These securities are owned by the clients, but the bank continues to manage the accounts. The banks clearly benefit from this, for they can reduce the size of their balance sheets – and the accompanying need for equity – and get rid of their responsibility for managing their balance-sheet risks, while continuing to earn a management commission. The de-risking strategies pursued today by banks and insurance companies raise two different ethical questions:

- The first concerns fiduciary duty, and clients' ability to understand the nature of the risks they will now be bearing, and the availability of operational resources. The size of the clients' account limits their scope for diversification or – as in the case of investment funds – increases their costs. This means that after de-risking by banks or insurance companies the risk/reward profile of the client's portfolio may change without him knowing why.

- The second concerns the role of banks, particularly retail banks, and the basic service they claim to provide. In systematically transferring the risk to their clients, banks make clear that they are changing not only their business model but also their social role. They are effectively withdrawing from their role as an absorber of financial shocks, which is not a neutral posture in terms of social ethics.

This brief review of ethical dilemmas in finance has by no means exhausted the issue. At most, it has shown the extent to which such dilemmas arise at the interface between technology and the institutional order, as well as aspirations and representations. In order to progress, ethics in finance therefore needs commitment from everyone and input from many disciplines.

Notes

1 Michel Albert, *Capitalism against Capitalism*, Le Seuil, Paris, 1991.
2 John Boatright (ed.), *Finance Ethics: Critical Issues in Theory and Practice*, Kolb Series in Finance, Wiley, Hoboken, 2010. This book, which contains articles by English-speaking authors, does not mention the issue of conflicting interests as such – a typical feature of the Anglo-Saxon tradition which, unlike the Rhine tradition, remains sceptical about the notion of fiduciary duty.
3 Tamar Frankel, *Trust and Honesty: America's Business Culture at a Crossroad*, Oxford University Press, New York, 2006.
4 As it is effective since 1 April 2015 in the Netherlands.
5 http://nypost.com/2009/12/13/the-only-thing-useful-banks-have-invented-in-20-years-is-the-atm/.
6 Lewis, Michael, *Flash Boys: A Wall Street Revolt*, Norton & Company, New York, 2014.

6　New avenues for action

The final chapter of this book gets away from the immediate protagonists of finance – operators or users – to consider how all the parties concerned can acknowledge the existence of ethical dilemmas, and the need to find ways of solving them.

The crisis that has erupted after three decades of euphoria and arrogance in the world of finance has clearly revealed its paradoxical situation. It has shown that the power of finance can shake the world economy to its foundations, and at the same time has exposed a whole list of intrinsic weaknesses in finance: weaknesses in balance sheets, in management teams and methods, gaps in regulation, biased representations, self-satisfaction, and superficial cultures and behaviour.

The many unkept promises have profoundly shaken society's trust in finance. Although the technical failings were identified almost at once, the necessary repairs and reforms are taking a long time, whether in individuals, in institutions, or in macroregulation. There is still a great deal of resistance from those who hope for a return to 'business as usual' – but this seems less and less likely as the years pass.[1]

The main diagnoses of the crisis were couched in technical, accounting, legal or regulatory terms, and largely overlooked the ethical dimension. This is not the first time that the ethical dimension of crises has been concealed, deliberately or otherwise. Back in 1948, François Perroux warned of the inevitable weakening of 'mental structures' during periods of great prosperity. At the very start of the Thirty Glorious Years, in an early volume of France's *Que sais-je?* series of booklets, on the subject of capitalism, Perroux wrote: 'There is always a more or less durable framework of pre-existing moral values within which a capitalist economy operates, values which may be quite alien to capitalism itself. But as the economy expands, its very success threatens this framework; capitalist values replace all others in the public esteem, and the preference for comfort and material well-being begins to erode the traditional institutions and mental patterns which are the basis of the social order. In a word, capitalism corrupts and corrodes. It uses up society's vital life-blood, yet is unable to replenish it.'[2] Similar warnings have been given since then, particularly by the philosopher-financier George Soros in the opening years of the millennium.[3]

In the first chapter of this book, the origins of financial euphoria and the subsequent financialisation of society were discussed with the help of multimodal causality. The same approach will be used here in conclusion to identify, at each level of causality, avenues for action that may reconcile society, the 'real' economy and finance. The goal is not simply to reverse the process and 'definancialise' what has been over-financialised, but to identify ways of restoring prudence, that is realism, to the financial sector.

The first stage of this process involves recognising that ethical dilemmas in finance are legitimate, and urgently need to be acknowledged and tackled. However, as analysed in the introduction, the dilemma is a moment of withdrawal and reflection, but is only justified by the action that it leads to and sheds light on. The second stage therefore involves identifying avenues for action with reference to the various 'causes' of the multimodal analysis.

6.1 Curbing expectations and aspirations in finance

During the Thirty Euphoric Years, finance gradually took on the social task of balancing amounts, due dates and risks. In this period, users of finance – savers, fund users or initiators of projects – multiplied. Finance thus became everyone's business and a 'jack of all trades', especially in performing tasks that had previously been carried out by non-financial methods and techniques. This growing trust created increasingly high – not to say excessive – expectations with regard to security of pensions (with corresponding risk transfers and promises of rewards), volumes of debts and loans, and financing of increasingly remote and improbable promises.

This transfer of tasks to finance took place amid a general fascination with the new techniques, and with only a few marginals prompting the ethical questions that the most basic prudence would have demanded.

Dazzled by illusory prospects of a brighter future, the whole of society – households, businesses and public bodies – began living on credit. In many parts of the world – above all the aging West – the production of debts, and hence receivables, became a sport, as if the headlong flight could last forever. Financial techniques maintained this illusion, but its source must be sought elsewhere: in the cultural development of consumer society towards an I-want-it-all-and-I-want-it-now attitude. Refusal to accept risks in the present resulted in their massive transfer to, and exponential accumulation in, the future – until the system, unexpectedly, reached the limits of its resistance in 2007.[4]

Although the loss – so evident in the contemporary world – of ethical references, of concern for the accomplished life, for others and for just institutions, is not entirely due to finance, it has no doubt been spurred on by financial promises. Finance is thus often accused of wrongdoing for which it is not in fact directly responsible.

The topic of this book is not 'financial ethics', but 'ethics in finance'. This way of stating the problem shows that ethics goes beyond finance, which is certainly a field in which it is applied, but is never its source. According to Ricœur's aforementioned definition, ethics is a posture that people acquire in all circumstances of their lives, whether political, economic, interpersonal, public or strictly private. This stresses anthropological unity and opposes the notion that in both social and individual life we should think in terms of independent spheres, each with its own ethics. The issue here is an anthropological one: integrated, internally coherent man, capable of his own ethical judgements, is contrasted with man fragmented into numerous roles or functions, each of which imposes on him a circumstantial ethics that is limited to a particular context – such as finance or business ethics – and hence is ultimately external to him.

The first series of actions involves reconsidering, in the light of prudence and ethics, Western societies' financial aspirations and expectations. Which promises, commitments and gambles can responsibly be made with regard to personal convictions, technical possibilities and alternatives, and with regard to social norms?

The revision of financial expectations should lead users of financial services to consider alternative ways of carrying out tasks hitherto entrusted to finance, and to resort to finance only when there is no alternative.

We must first distinguish between risks we can or should bear ourselves, and those we should entrust to financial management through savings. Reduction of transferred risks presupposes the activation of other channels for risk management: acquisition of goods and skills that can be used in the long term, activation of informal reciprocity, intergenerational solidarity, neighbourly relations and those provided by community life. After the large-scale demutualisation brought about by finance, the time has come to create new, extra financial, ways of mutualising risks.

The same reasoning applied to the use of financial resources should lead to a reduction in demand for loans for 'everything and anything', which burdens the future without changing the present. This should make more funding available for truly promising projects, in small as well as large businesses. In medium-sized businesses, self-financing should gradually replace the pursuit of leverage and dividends.

There is increasing experience of solidarity, sustainability and ethics-based finance. This offers a middle way between the normality inherited from the euphoric years and the personal assumption of risk. Such initiatives, funds or labels involve making users of financial services think in terms of more than just classic risk and reward. Sharing of resources and income, personal involvement in how savings are used by others and the launching of economic activities through direct funding are among the possible ways of helping fund users to update their financial expectations.

This back-to-reality process involves revising promises and commitments, which may sometimes be painful and cause losses of both money and illusions, particularly in the case of life insurance or pensions. Yet this is the price Western society will have to pay for having succumbed to the financial improbable promises.[5] The issue of social ethics, which will have to be faced sooner or later, involves knowing how this burden should be distributed, since grave errors of judgement have been made by politicians, institutions and private individuals.

6.2 Enhancing the importance of personal relationships

The development of world financial organisation towards the financial-market model has led to an exponential expansion in financial transactions, often at the expense of personal relationships between parties to financial relations, namely intermediaries and their clients.

The discussion in the opening chapters emphasised the importance of 'others' in ethical thinking. Once they are concealed by an algorithm or the faceless mass, ethics is on thin ice. A return to the ethical dilemma in finance thus means rediscovering the importance of more personal relationships with users. The efforts now being made within businesses to achieve asymmetrically personal relationships with clients are a very imperfect response to this emergency. They involve creating very precise and efficient computerised client profiles, so that any employee can make clients feel they are in a personal relationship – whereas in fact it is nothing of the kind. Although the business 'knows' its client, the employees who deal with the various aspects of their files – often on purpose – do not; and in the absence of a human face, empathy – so effective in identifying ethical dilemmas – is unlikely to develop.

A return to true person-to-person relationships, which is essential if a sense of ethical responsibility is to grow, conflicts with certain current managerial practices that aim to increase mobility of employees and depersonalise tasks and skills so that the business is less dependent on its personnel. This tendency – which is justified by considerations of short-term profitability – helps to uproot concern for ethics within the business. Such choices by boards of directors may eventually leave the business ethically blind or, worse, autistic. Symptoms of these grave developments – which are replacing relationships with transactions, and involve deliberate abdication of ethics and ex-ante responsibility – can be seen not only in financial businesses.

The development of more personal relationships in the finance sector should lead to the emergence of true partnerships which will also involve fairer distribution of risks. Asymmetry of risks is particularly striking in debt relationships. The development of financing instruments that correct this asymmetry without entirely eliminating it is another promising way to make relationships more personal. An example is the 'profit and loss sharing' business financing model.[6] In order to become a reality, such initiatives depend on the revision of legislation that currently imposes a sharp distinction between debt and equity participation.

6.3 Simplifying the way finance works

Beyond its material and formal dimensions, it is time to look at the efficient cause of financialisation, especially the institutions that perform the threefold intermediation process referred to earlier and which have been the main divers of financialisation. There are four avenues for action in their organisation and management that may make them more susceptible to ethics:

- The first concerns their size and complexity. In 2011 the Financial Stability Board started to publish a list of some thirty banks as global systemically important financial institutions, using four criteria: their size, their interconnection with the other components of the global financial system, their internal complexity and their near-monopoly in certain areas of activity. More than the other three criteria, the one that deserves attention here is internal complexity. In a complex business, activities are so closely interwoven that management becomes a problem, since decision-makers are unable to assess properly all the consequences of their acts. This greatly limits the range of responsibility or ethical considerations. Actors who cannot perceive or anticipate the consequences of their decisions cannot be expected to behave responsibly ex-ante.

  The complexity of organisations must therefore be reduced so that they can perceive ethical dilemmas. Size and complexity are not necessarily corollaries. Some vast businesses are so simply organised that they can be understood, particularly by regulators, and can be managed responsibly. The simplification process is an essentially thankless one, for it involves giving up and merging activities that directly affect employees. This is an urgent task, in order to reduce systemic risk and make organisations ethically more responsive.

- The second factor is veracity, which derives from the need for simplicity. This is particularly necessary in the present context, in which global conglomerates that advocate to provide all services are increasingly impossible to define in terms of their core business. The client should be able, and should want, to know as unambiguously as possible what kind of financial operator he is dealing with. Traditional banks, savings banks, hedge funds or brokers appeal to different clients, with different expectations and profiles. The speed of changes and mergers increases the importance of financial operator's duty to care about the real-time veracity of his image. This is particularly necessary and demanding because, thanks to communication and marketing techniques, an institution's image and reputation tend to have a life of its own, regardless of its business reality. Operators therefore have a duty to show themselves to their clients and partners as they really are. If client relationships are to be based on trust, the image must match reality.
- The third factor is remuneration and incentives within financial institutions. The incentive system is not neutral; it spurs employees towards behaviours and attitudes that are preferable in terms of the business's performance and strategy. Incentives are therefore a highly sensitive aspect of management, for they may encourage people to ignore ethical dilemmas or distort the way employees solve such dilemmas. A return to ethics depends on these incentive systems being aligned with two basic principles. First, the incentive method must not induce employees to deceive clients or partners, or to favour some over others. Second, incentives must not induce employees to seek remunerations other than those deriving from the contract. This means that information concerning inducements by third parties must be clearly displayed.

  The remuneration system must be geared to the client's best interests, even if this may impair the institution's performance – a basic requirement for any activity that seeks, like finance, to serve the client. Yet it remains difficult to apply in conglomerates with varied, interdependent activities. The need for integrity in remuneration is thus an additional argument for simplifying it.
- The fourth factor is the culture of financial institutions. The scandals brought to light by the financial crisis have shown just how small a role ethical dilemmas have played in the cultures of the world's leading financial players. Corporate culture does not stop at codes or charters or corporate values set out in reports or on websites, but extends to the way in which these values are actually perceived by employees – for it is they who are in direct contact with clients and partners, and it is what they do and say that reflects the business's true culture.[7]

Culture plays the same part in businesses as in daily life: it is made up of previously acquired habits and reflexes. The distinction between habits and *habitus*, that is good habits, which was mentioned in the first chapter should be recalled here. A culture based on ethics permeates the business with 'good habits', which eventually become automatic reflexes. These are essential, particularly in situations that require employees to make choices which involve simultaneously several values. The 'Mind the Gap' approach mentioned in the first chapter comes into its own here. Where ethical dilemmas are acknowledged by the culture, employees will not be reluctant to talk about them to colleagues or superiors and to jointly seek a solution. Like a virtuous circle, this further enriches the corporate culture.

A corporate culture geared to ethics requires a special effort from managers, for they must listen to their employees' dilemmas. Such an exercise, though it may be potentially destabilising, is essential, for a culture is not decreed – it is assimilated, but only if it is in harmony with everyone's ethical goals. A living, solid corporate culture is thus the best guarantee that the business will not be dragged down by the blindness of a few. Such a culture must find an appropriate way of responding to warning signals and providing whistle-blowers a framework combining responsibility and security they need.

6.4 Teaching finance differently

The strength and coherence of the scientific paradigm gave financial euphoria both a conceptual framework and scientific legitimacy. The crisis has revealed the limitations of the financial world view and the gaps in the paradigm. Yet, despite such crystal-clear empirical evidence, the way in which finance is taught at universities has hardly changed. There are three urgently needed updates:

- Just like economic theory, from which it emerged, financial-market theory is based on a reductionist view of human beings. 'Economic man' (*homo oeconomicus*) is the embodiment of a hedonistic rationality algorithm. Faced with a choice, he systematically opts for the alternatives that give him the highest degree of satisfaction or utility. He will behave similarly with regard to risk and reward. The great advantage of this model is its formal coherence – but at the cost of oversimplification that ignores human beings' altruistic, emotional dimension, which is incidentally the focus of the current interest in 'behavioural' finance. However, a sense of realism requires that the limitations of models built on such fragile hypotheses, and the conclusions drawn from them, should at least be criticised in the light of a more realistic view of human nature that is sensitive to the ethical aspects of his deeds.

- Financial theory completely ignores the 'real' economy – just as economic theory ignores finance. Bridges need to be built, at the level of macro analysis and at the level of individual behaviour and institutional choices, in order to grasp both facets of one and the same economic/ financial reality in businesses, households and public bodies.
- The explicitly ethical dimension must shed light on both the hypotheses and the conclusions of financial models built on solely technical premises. This must be done in an interdisciplinary manner, with input from sociology, economics, philosophy and epistemology, and the results made available to finance students.

6.5 Ethics as a goal

The ethical dilemma arises when alternative behaviours are gauged against higher goals, such as Ricœur's 'accomplished life'. It is by taking this injunction seriously that the ethical dilemmas outlined in this book have been revealed. Opening up to ethics therefore depends on moving beyond the more-more-more attitude. This recalls the precepts of all the world's philosophies, which see the acceptance of frugality as the acme of human endeavour.

Without going that far, finance must return to the goal of any tertiary activity, which is to serve – that is to respond to clients' needs, making the best of the available technical resources. During the Thirty Euphoric Years, finance sold all manner of illusions; now the time has come for it to examine its true capabilities in light of its recent rude awakening, and consider what kind of service it can really provide. This exercise in realism should also involve regulatory bodies, whose task it will be to decide what level of systemic risk society can still bear.

In conclusion, taking ethics in finance seriously should lead to a reduction in the volume of its activity, by reducing both supply and demand. This may be painful for what is currently a highly overinflated sector. Yet this is the price that must be paid for the unavoidable structural adjustment and the reinvention of a financial sector that can realistically and truly serve the highest aspirations of man and society.

Notes

1 See in particular the first chapter of the 2009 Annual Report by the Bank of International Settlements (BIS), which in a matter of pages paints a clear and ruthless picture of what went wrong.
2 Francois Perroux, *Le capitalisme*, Que sais-je?, no 315, PUF, Paris, 1948.

3 Soros, George, *The Crisis of Global Capitalism*, Little, Brown and Company, New York, 1998.

4 Étienne Perrot, *Refus du risque et catastrophes financières*, Salvator, Paris, 2011.

5 Nassim Nicholas Taleb's famous book *The Black Swan: The Impact of the Highly Improbable* (Random House, London, 2007) reminds us that, just like black swans, rare events such as the financial crisis can never be ruled out, even though they are not predicted by probabilistic models.

6 Bertrand du Marais and Stanislas Ordody, 'Une nouvelle approche du financement des entreprises: le principe du partage des profits et pertes', in *Rapport moral sur l'argent dans le monde 2013*, Association d'économie financière, Paris, 2013; www.aef.asso.fr.

7 See Group of 30, Banking Conduct and Culture, A Call for Sustained and Comprehensive Reform, Washington, July 2015; http://group30.org/images/uploads/publications/G30_BankingConductandCulture.pdf.

Bibliography

Albert, Michel, *Capitalism Against Capitalism*, Whurr Publishers, London, 1993.

Ansotegui, Carmen, Gómez-Bezares, Fernando, and González Fabre, Raúl, *Ética de las Finanzas*, Desclée de Brouwer, Bilbao, 2015.

Assouly, Judith, *Morale ou Finance ? La déontologie dans les pratiques financières*, Les presses de Sciences Po, Paris, 2013.

Badaracco, Joseph L. J., *Defining Moments: When Managers Must Choose between Right and Right*, Harvard Business School Press, Boston, MA, 1997.

Becchetti, Leonardo, *Il denaro fa la felicità?*, GLF Editori, Lateza, Bari, 2007.

Boatright, John (ed.), *Finance Ethics: Critical Issues in Theory and Practice*, Kolb Series in Finance, Wiley, Hoboken, NJ, 2010.

Bourguinat, Henri and Briys, Eric, *L'arrogance de la finance*, La Découverte, Paris, 2009.

Cosgrove-Sacks, Carol and Dembinski, Paul H. (eds), *Trust and Ethics in Finance: Innovative Ideas from the Robin Cosgrove Prize*, Globethics, Geneva, 2012.

De Lauzun, Pierre, *La finance peut-elle être au service de l'homme?*, Desclée de Brouwer, Paris, 2015.

Dembinski, Paul H., *Finance: Servant or Deceiver? Financialisation at the Crossroads*, Palgrave Macmillan, London, 2008.

Dembinski, Paul H. (ed.), *Pratiques financières – regards chrétiens*, Desclée de Brouwer, Paris, 2009.

Dembinski, Paul H., Bonvin, Jean-Michel, Dommen, Edouard, Monnet, François-Marie, 'Ethics Foundations of Responsible Investment', *Journal of Business Ethics*, vol. 48: 203–213, 2003.

Dherse, Jean-Loup and Minguet, Hugues, *L'Éthique ou le Chaos?*, Presses de la Renaissance, Paris, 1999.

Dobson, John, *Finance Ethics: The Rationality of Virtue*, Rowman & Littlefield, Oxford, 1997.

Frankel, Tamar, *Trust and Honesty: America's Business Culture at a Crossroad*, Oxford University Press, New York, 2006.

Giraud, Pierre-Noël, *Le commerce des promesses: petit traité sur la finance moderne*, Denoël, Paris, 2001.

Goodpaster, Kenneth, *Conscience and Corporate Culture*, Wiley-Blackwell, Oxford, 2007.

Group of 30, *Banking Conduct and Culture, A Call for Sustained and Comprehensive Reform*, Washington, July 2015, http://group30.org/images/uploads/publica tions/G30_BankingConductandCulture.pdf.

Hayek, Friedrich, *Denationalisation of Money*, Institute for International Affairs, London, 1976.

Hayek, Friedrich, 'Toward Free Market Money', *Wall Street Journal*, 19 August 1977.

Hemel, Ulrich, Fritzsche, Andreas and Manemann, Jürgen (eds), *Habituelle Unternehmensethik: von der Ethik zum Ethos*, Nomos, Baden-Baden, 2012.

Hendry, John, *Ethics and Finance: An Introduction*, Cambridge University Press, Cambridge, 2013.

Hirschman, Albert, *Exit, Voice and Loyalty: Response to Decline in Firms, Organizations and States*, Harvard University Press, Cambridge, MA, 1970.

Ingarden, Roman, *Über die Verantwortung: ihre ontischen Fundamente*, Reclam, Stuttgart, 1970.

Jonas, Hans, *The Imperative of Responsibility: In Search of an Ethics for the Technological Age*, University of Chicago Press, Chicago, IL, 1984 (first published in German in 1979).

Koslowski, Peter,*The Ethics of Banking: Conclusions from the Financial Crisis*, Springer Netherlands, 2011.

Lacroix, André and Marchildon, Allison, *Quelle éthique pour la finance? Portrait et analyse de la finance socialement responsable*, Presses Universitaires du Québec, Québec, 2013.

Lear, Jonathan, *Aristotle: The Desire to Understand*, Cambridge University Press, Cambridge, 1997.

Lelièvre, Frédéric and Pilet, François, *Krach Machine*, Calmann-Lévy, Paris, 2013.

Lewis, Michael, *Flash Boys: A Wall Street Revolt*, Norton & Company, New York, 2014.

Marais, Bertrand du and Ordody, Stanislad, 'Une nouvelle approche du financement des entreprises: le principe du partage des profits et pertes', in *Rapport moral sur l'argent dans le monde 2013*, Association d'économie financière, Paris; www.aef.asso.fr.

Melé, Domènec, *Business Ethics in Action: Seeking Human Excellence in Organisations*, Houndmills, Basingstoke, Hampshire, Palgrave Macmillan, 2010.

Morris, Nicholas and Vines, David (eds), *Capital Failure: Rebuilding Trust in Financial Services*, Oxford University Press, Oxford, 2014.

Noonan, John Thomas, *The Scholastic Analysis of Usury*, Harvard University Press, Cambridge, MA, 1957.

Perrot, Étienne, *L'art de décider en situations complexes*, Desclée de Brouwer, Paris, 2007.

Perrot, Étienne, *Refus du risque et catastrophes financières*, Salvator, Paris, 2011.

Perrot, Étienne, *Le discernement managérial*, Desclée de Brouwer, Paris, 2012.

Perroux, Francois, *Le capitalisme*, Que sais-je?, no 315, PUF, Paris, 1948.

Plender, John, *Capitalism: Money, Morals and Markets*, Biteback Publishing, London, 2016.

Pons-Vignon, Nicolas and Nuube, Phumzile, *Confronting Finance: Mobilizing the 99% for Economic and Social Progress,* International Labour Organization, Geneva, 2012.

Puel, Hugues, *Une éthique pour l'économie: ethos, crises, choix*, Éditions du Cerf, Collection Recherches morales, Paris, 2010.

Régnon, Théodore de, *La métaphysique des causes d'après Saint Thomas et Albert le Grand*, Victor Retaux Éditeur, Paris, 1906.

Reich, Robert, *The Work of Nations*, Vintage Press, New York, 1992.

Reifner, Udo, Clerc-Renaud, Sebastien and Knobloch, R.A. Michael, *Study on Interest Rate Restrictions in the EU*, Institut für Finanzdienstleistungen, Hamburg, 2009; http://ec.europa.eu/internal_market/finservices-retail/docs/credit/irr_report_en.pdf.

Ricœur, Paul, *Soi-même comme un autre*, Le Seuil, Paris, 1990.

Soros, George (1998), *The Crisis of Global Capitalism*, Little, Brown and Company, New York, 1998.

Taleb, Nassim Nicholas, *The Black Swan: The Impact of the Highly Improbable*, Random House, London, 2007.

Taylor, Gabrielle, *Deadly Vices*, Clarendon Press, Oxford, 2006.

Thévenoz, Luc and Bahar, Rashid (eds), *Conflicts of Interest: Corporate Governance and Financial Markets*, Kluwer Law International, Alphen aan den Rijn, 2007.

Villa, Jes, *Ethics in Banking: The Role of Moral Values and Judgements in Finance*, Houndmills, Basingstoke, Hampshire Palgrave Macmillan, 2015.

Weber, M. 'Politics as a Vocation'. In *From Max Weber: Essays in Sociology* (pp. 77–128), ed. and trans. H. H. Gerth and C. Wright Mills, New York: Oxford University Press, 1946.

Welby, Justin, *Can Companies Sin? 'Whether', 'How' and 'Who' in Company Accountability*, Grove Books, Cambridge, 1992.

Winiger, Bénédict, *Verantwortung, Reversibilität und Verschulden*, Mohr Siebeck, Tübingen, 2013.

Zak, Paul, J., *Moral Markets: The Critical Role of Values in the Economy*, Princeton University Press, Woodstock, 2008.

Index

accomplished life 23, 29, 42, 67
accounting 47–8
allocation: of capital 16, 53; of risk 15, 53, 59
arbitrage 37, 46, 51
Aristotle 10, 19
asymmetry: of information 46–9, 56, 62; of risk 69; of understanding 56, 57, 60

bank 45, 47, 53–4, 63–4, 70
bankruptcy 50

Calvin, Jean 35
Cantillon, Richard 42
capitalism 66
cash 27, 63
causality, multimodal 11–17, 21, 66
cause: efficient 11, 69; exemplary 11, 13, 69; final 11, 16, 69; formal 11, 13, 69; material 10, 12
charter 70
Christianity 27, 34, 40
community 21, 46, 61–2, 67
complexity 5, 69
compliance 60
conflict of interest 3, 25, 56, 58
corporate culture 5, 70; finance 14
credit 12, 34, 43, 47, 51, 66

debt 25, 34–6, 40–2, 45–7, 50–1
decision 25, 29, 41
demutualisation 12, 13, 33, 61, 67

derivatives 9, 59, 63
Dherse, Jean-Loup 24
dilemma 21–7 68, 69, 70; of fund holders 27–40; of fund users 40–56, of intermediaries 58–65
discount rate 44, 45

epistemology 4, 72
ethical autism and alienation 5
ethics 4, 16, 17–19, 20–6, 36, 37; applied 17; business 67; fundamental 17; social 7, 33, 38, 50, 64, 68
euphoria see Thirty Euphoric Years

family 10, 28, 41, 43
fiduciary 10, 13, 57, 63
financial: assets 9, 29, 34, 37, 58; crisis of 2007 1, 65, 70; market economy 54; innovation 59; intermediation 9, 12, 16, 25, 42, 53–65, 69; returns 30; sector 16, 71; services 10; techniques 12
Financial Stability Board 9
financialisation 11, 16, 36, 40, 66, 69
foreign currency 46, 61
Friedman, Milton 14
frugality 28, 72
fund users 40–6

gamble 8, 35–6, 42, 46, 50, 67
greed 39
guarantee 3, 38, 47, 50

habitus 22, 23, 71
harmony 18–19
herd behaviour 48
high–frequency trading 14, 62
homo oeconomicus 18, 71

IMF 51
impact 24, 31, 32
insider trading 60–2
institution 18, 21, 24, 64
insurance 27–8, 33, 35, 68
integrity 57, 60
interest 34–5, 44, 49, 62
intergenerational 29, 67
intertemporal 29, 40
investment : fund 9, 16, 39; project
    16, 41, 44–5; public 41, 45–6;
    responsible 20, 28; risk 32, 55, 58
Islam 34

Jubilee 35, 51
Judaism 34, 35
judgement 47–9, 67

law 18, 20, 22, 29, 48, 50
legal person 20, 42, 50
leverage 43, 44, 67
liberalism 14
Libor 61
liquidity 15, 27, 29
loan *see* credit and debt
Long-Term Capital Management 1

macro 27, 38, 42, 50–3, 65, 72
management: of assets 27, 37, 58–60;
    of risks 16, 37, 63, 67
market 7, 5, 61; efficient 15, 36, 55, 61;
    finance 4, 14, 16; integrity 27, 60–2;
    society 36
Markowitz, Harry 14, 63
meso 7, 46
micro 7, 18, 49, 61
microfinance 49
Mind the GAP 24, 25, 71
Modigliani–Miller theorem 44

money 9, 10, 36, 42, 50
moral 5, 17, 20, 27, 34–6, 57, 65;
    hazard 10; judgement 2; law 3, 17,
    22, 27; norms 1
moralists 3, 22, 41
mortgages, subprime 42

payments 16, 25
pensions 27, 33, 38, 66, 68
performance 23, 24, 33
politics *see* public
price 22, 36, 37, 55, 59, 63; quality of
    61–3
product 7, 29, 30, 31, 39, 59; structured
    9, 48, 60; synthetic 9
professions 7, 49, 54–8, 60, 65
promise 8–12, 16, 38–40, 50, 66–8
property 27
Protestantism 28
prudence 4, 6, 42, 67
public 1–6, 38, 55; authority 10, 33;
    bodies 12, 24–5, 40, 47–8, 50, 66, 27;
    debtors 40–50; finance 45; funds 16,
    45, 45–6; promise 10; trust 10

quality: intrinsic of action 24; of price
    61–3

rating agency 48
real economy 15, 63, 66, 72
reciprocity 12, 18, 67
regulator, regulation 6–10, 25, 48, 55,
    59–65, 72
relation 13–19, 68–70
remuneration 3, 45, 58, 70
rentier 25, 27–40
responsibility 5–6, 17–23, 27, 30, 43,
    63, 71; direct 54; ethical 20, 49, 68;
    ex-ante 19–21, 60, 69; ex-post
    19–21; legal 20; material 29;
    paternalistic 54; social 31–2, 50;
    ultimate 54
Ricoeur, Paul 17–24, 30, 67, 72
risk 3, 12, 15, 33–5, 38, 41–9;
    distribution of 54–5, 69; investment

32; management 16, 37–8, 63, 67; systemic 6, 69, 72; take risks 22, 30; transfer 60, 63, 66–7
risk/reward paradigm 4, 9, 10, 15–16, 30, 60–8, 71

savings 12, 27–8, 30, 33, 36, 38, 39
scandal 2, 70
shareholder 32–6, 43–6
solidarity 12, 67
speculation 9, 36, 42
standards 49, 59
state *see* public
supervision 9, 38, 50, 59
sustainability 31, 32, 67
systemic: importance 1, 6; risk 6, 69, 72; transformation 1
systemically important financial institutions 55, 69

technology 5, 16, 55, 64, 66
theory of finance 4, 14, 56, 59, 68, 71
Thirty Euphoric Years 2, 5–6, 12, 16, 35–9, 59, 65–6, 72
Thirty Glorious Years 2, 65
transaction 3, 9, 13, 22, 61
transdisciplinary 11, 72
transparency 58
trust 2–3, 12–13, 33, 36–7, 43, 46, 58, 65–6, 70

uncertainty 3, 15
usury 49–50, 70

value 10, 14, 18–22, 30, 36, 43, 48
virtue 18–22, 36
volatility 37, 63

Weber, Max 19

 Taylor & Francis eBooks

Helping you to choose the right eBooks for your Library

Add Routledge titles to your library's digital collection today. Taylor and Francis ebooks contains over 50,000 titles in the Humanities, Social Sciences, Behavioural Sciences, Built Environment and Law.

Choose from a range of subject packages or create your own!

Benefits for you
- » Free MARC records
- » COUNTER-compliant usage statistics
- » Flexible purchase and pricing options
- » All titles DRM-free.

Benefits for your user
- » Off-site, anytime access via Athens or referring URL
- » Print or copy pages or chapters
- » Full content search
- » Bookmark, highlight and annotate text
- » Access to thousands of pages of quality research at the click of a button.

REQUEST YOUR **FREE** INSTITUTIONAL TRIAL TODAY

Free Trials Available
We offer free trials to qualifying academic, corporate and government customers.

eCollections – Choose from over 30 subject eCollections, including:

Archaeology	Language Learning
Architecture	Law
Asian Studies	Literature
Business & Management	Media & Communication
Classical Studies	Middle East Studies
Construction	Music
Creative & Media Arts	Philosophy
Criminology & Criminal Justice	Planning
Economics	Politics
Education	Psychology & Mental Health
Energy	Religion
Engineering	Security
English Language & Linguistics	Social Work
Environment & Sustainability	Sociology
Geography	Sport
Health Studies	Theatre & Performance
History	Tourism, Hospitality & Events

For more information, pricing enquiries or to order a free trial, please contact your local sales team:
www.tandfebooks.com/page/sales

 Routledge
Taylor & Francis Group

The home of
Routledge books

www.tandfebooks.com

For Product Safety Concerns and Information please contact our EU
representative GPSR@taylorandfrancis.com Taylor & Francis Verlag GmbH,
Kaufingerstraße 24, 80331 München, Germany

Printed and bound by CPI Group (UK) Ltd, Croydon, CR0 4YY
11/04/2025
01844009-0008